IFRS® Stand...

**required for accounting periods
beginning on or after 1 January 2021,
excluding changes not yet required**

This edition is issued in three parts

PART A

contains the text of IFRS Standards including IAS® Standards,
IFRIC® Interpretations and SIC® Interpretations, together with
the *Conceptual Framework for Financial Reporting*
(Glossary included)

See also Parts B and C of this edition:

Part B

*contains the illustrative examples and implementation guidance
that accompany the Standards, together with
IFRS practice statements*

Part C

*contains the bases for conclusions that accompany the
Standards, the* Conceptual Framework for Financial
Reporting *and IFRS practice statements, together with
the* Constitution *and* Due Process Handbook *of the IFRS
Foundation*

Contents

continued...

IFRIC Interpretations

continued...

...continued

Introduction to this edition

The International Accounting Standards Board

The International Accounting Standards Board (Board) is the standard-setting body of the IFRS® Foundation (Foundation). Appointed, overseen and funded by the Foundation, the Board has complete responsibility for technical matters, including the preparation and issuing of IFRS Standards. The Trustees of the IFRS Foundation (Trustees) are responsible for governance and oversight. The IFRS Foundation Monitoring Board provides a formal link between the Trustees and public authorities in order to enhance the public accountability of the Foundation.

IFRS Standards

IFRS Standards (Standards) are mandatory pronouncements and comprise:

(a)   IFRS Standards;

(b)   IAS® Standards; and

(c)   Interpretations developed by the IFRS Interpretations Committee (IFRIC® Interpretations) or its predecessor body, the Standing Interpretations Committee (SIC® Interpretations).

Standards are issued after formal due process and financial statements must not be described as complying with IFRS Standards unless they comply with all the requirements of the Standards.

The requirements of a Standard, including any appendices setting out mandatory application guidance, are usually accompanied by non-mandatory material, including:

(a)   a basis for conclusions, which summarises the Board's main considerations when it was developing the Standard;

(b)   dissenting opinions, if any, by individual Board members who voted against the publication of the Standard or amendment to the Standard;

(c)   implementation guidance; and

(d)   illustrative examples.

The rubric following the contents page of each Standard sets out the authority of the information contained in or accompanying that Standard.

The title page of each Standard details its history.

Each new Standard and amendment to a Standard sets out its effective date and may contain transition provisions. When the Board issues new Standards or amendments to Standards it generally allows an entity to apply the new requirements before their effective date.

What does this edition contain?

This edition contains only Standards issued by the Board as at 31 December 2020 that are required for accounting periods beginning on or after 1 January 2021 (that is all Standards with an effective date on or before 1 January 2021).

Standards and amendments to Standards issued by 31 December 2020 with an effective date after 1 January 2021, are excluded from this edition and will be included in *IFRS® Standards — Issued at 1 January 2021* and in *The Annotated IFRS® Standards — Standards issued at 1 January 2021*.

Publications and translations

The Foundation holds the copyright for IFRS Standards, IAS Standards, IFRIC Interpretations, SIC Interpretations, exposure drafts, discussion papers and other Board publications in all countries, except where the Foundation has expressly waived the right to enforce copyright on portions of that material. For more information regarding the Foundation's copyrights, please refer to the copyright notice with this edition or on the website at www.ifrs.org.

IFRS Standards have been translated into a number of languages. The Foundation considers additional translations as needs arise. For more information, contact the Translation, Adoption and Copyright team on tac@ifrs.org.

More information

The Foundation's website, www.ifrs.org, provides news, updates and other resources related to the Board and the Foundation. The latest publications and subscription services can be ordered from the Foundation's webshop at shop.ifrs.org.

For more information about the Foundation, or to obtain copies of its publications and details of the Foundation's subscription services, visit the website or write to:

IFRS Foundation
Publications Department
Columbus Building
7 Westferry Circus
Canary Wharf
London E14 4HD
United Kingdom

Telephone: +44 (0)20 7332 2730
Email: publications@ifrs.org
Website: www.ifrs.org

Changes in this edition

This section is a brief guide to the changes incorporated in this 2021 edition since the publication of IFRS® Standards — Required at 1 January 2020.

Basis of preparation

This edition contains only IFRS Standards issued by the International Accounting Standards Board (Board) as at 31 December 2020 that are required for accounting periods beginning on or after 1 January 2021 (that is, all Standards with an effective date on or before 1 January 2021).

Standards and amendments to Standards issued by 31 December 2020 but with an effective date after 1 January 2021 are excluded from this edition; they will be reproduced in IFRS® Standards — Issued at 1 January 2021 and in The Annotated IFRS® Standards — Standards issued at 1 January 2021.

New in this edition

The following pronouncements are effective from 1 January 2021 and included in this edition:

- a revised version of the Constitution and Due Process Handbook of the IFRS Foundation;

- Annual Improvements to IFRS Standards 2018–2020 — amendments to IFRS 16 Leases;

- Covid-19-Related Rent Concessions — amendment to IFRS 16;

- Extension of the Temporary Exemption from Applying IFRS 9 — amendments to IFRS 4 Insurance Contracts; and

- Interest Rate Benchmark Reform — Phase 2 — amendments to IFRS 4, IFRS 7 Financial Instruments: Disclosures, IFRS 9 Financial Instruments, IFRS 16 and IAS 39 Financial Instruments: Recognition and Measurement.

The following table provides the publication and effective dates of these pronouncements. The *Amendments to Standards* section provides further details of these pronouncements.

New requirements effective from 1 January 2021				
Standard/ amendment	When issued	Effective date (early application is possible unless otherwise noted)	Standards/ Interpretations amended	Standard withdrawn
Annual Improvements to IFRS Standards 2018–2020	May 2020	Takes effect immediately	IFRS 16	
Covid-19-Related Rent Concessions Amendment to IFRS 16	May 2020	1 June 2020	IFRS 16	
Extension of the Temporary Exemption from Applying IFRS 9 Amendments to IFRS 4	June 2020	25 June 2020	IFRS 4	
Interest Rate Benchmark Reform— Phase 2 Amendments to IFRS 9, IAS 39, IFRS 7, IFRS 4 and IFRS 16	August 2020	1 January 2021	IFRS 4, IFRS 7, IFRS 9, IFRS 16; IAS 39	

The Glossary has been revised. Minor editorial corrections to Standards (including necessary updating) have also been made; a list of all such corrections is available at www.ifrs.org.

New and revised Standards, Interpretations and practice statements are available to eIFRS subscribers at eifrs.ifrs.org.

Constitution and *Due Process Handbook* of the IFRS Foundation

The *Due Process Handbook* was revised following a review by the Trustees' Due Process Oversight Committee (DPOC) to ensure it remains fit for purpose and continues to reflect good practice.

The main changes were to:

- clarify the authority of agenda decisions published by the Interpretations Committee and their role in supporting consistent application of IFRS Standards, and to enhance the related due process by formally involving the Board in their finalisation; and

- reflect recent developments in the Board's process for assessing the likely effects of a new or amended IFRS Standard.

In addition, the amendments enhance and streamline the consultation requirements for adding major projects to the Board's work plan; update and enhance the minimum amount of review required for educational material produced by the IFRS Foundation; and clarify the DPOC's role in overseeing the IFRS Taxonomy due process.

Resulting from the amendments to the *Due Process Handbook*, an amendment was also made to the IFRS Foundation Constitution. This amendment reflects that the Advisory Council advises the Board (and Trustees) on strategic matters and no longer functions as a technical consultative body.

Amendments to Standards

Annual Improvements to IFRS Standards 2018–2020

Annual Improvements to IFRS Standards 2018–2020 amended an illustrative example accompanying IFRS 16 *Leases*.

Covid-19-Related Rent Concessions

Covid-19-Related Rent Concessions, which amends IFRS 16, is effective from 1 June 2020 with earlier application permitted. The amendment permits lessees, as a practical expedient, not to assess whether rent concessions that occur as a direct consequence of the covid-19 pandemic and meet specified conditions are lease modifications and, instead, to account for those rent concessions as if they were not lease modifications.

Extension of the Temporary Exemption from Applying IFRS 9

Extension of the Temporary Exemption from Applying IFRS 9, which amends IFRS 4, extends the temporary exemption from applying IFRS 9 by two years. It will expire for annual reporting periods beginning on or after 1 January 2023.

Interest Rate Benchmark Reform—Phase 2

Interest Rate Benchmark Reform – Phase 2 (Phase 2 amendments) was issued in August 2020 and amends IFRS 9, IAS 39, IFRS 7, IFRS 4 and IFRS 16. The Phase 2 amendments address issues that might affect financial reporting during the reform of an interest rate benchmark, including the effects of changes to contractual cash flows or hedging relationships arising from the replacement of an interest rate benchmark with an alternative benchmark rate. The objectives of the Phase 2 amendments are to:

*   support companies in applying IFRS Standards when changes are made to contractual cash flows or hedging relationships because of the reform; and

*   assist companies in providing useful information to users of financial statements.

Disclosure of the possible impact of issued Standards that are not yet required

As explained above, this edition does not include Standards that have an effective date later than 1 January 2021.

These Standards are relevant, however, even if an entity does not intend to adopt a requirement early. Paragraph 30 of IAS 8 *Accounting Policies, Changes in Accounting Estimates and Errors* requires an entity to disclose 'information relevant to assessing the possible impact that application of the new IFRS [Standard] will have on the entity's financial statements in the period of initial application'.

The following table shows the new Standards and amendments to Standards that were issued by 1 January 2021 but which have an effective date after 1 January 2021.

Standards issued, but not effective, at 1 January 2021				
Standard/ amendment	When issued	Effective date (early application is possible unless otherwise noted)	Standards/ Interpretations amended	Standard withdrawn
Sale or Contribution of Assets Amendments to IFRS 10 and IAS 28	September 2014	Postponed indefinitely	IFRS 10; IAS 28	
IFRS 17 *Insurance Contracts*(a)	May 2017	1 January 2021	IFRS 1, IFRS 3, IFRS 3 (as amended by IFRS 16), IFRS 5, IFRS 7, IFRS 7 (as amended by IFRS 16), IFRS 9, IFRS 15; IAS 1, IAS 7, IAS 16, IAS 19, IAS 28, IAS 32, IAS 36, IAS 37, IAS 38, IAS 40; SIC 27	IFRS 4
Classification of Liabilities as Current or Non-current(b) Amendments to IAS 1	January 2020	1 January 2023	IAS 1	
Reference to the Conceptual Framework Amendments to IFRS 3	May 2020	1 January 2022	IFRS 3	
Onerous Contracts— Cost of Fulfilling a Contract Amendments to IAS 37	May 2020	1 January 2022	IAS 37	

continued...

...continued

Standards issued, but not effective, at 1 January 2021				
Standard/ amendment	When issued	Effective date (early application is possible unless otherwise noted)	Standards/ Interpretations amended	Standard withdrawn
Property, Plant and Equipment: Proceeds before Intended Use Amendments to IAS 16	May 2020	1 January 2022	IAS 16	
Annual Improvements to IFRS Standards 2018-2020	May 2020	1 January 2022	IFRS 1, IFRS 9; IAS 41	
Amendments to IFRS 17	June 2020	1 January 2023	IFRS 3, IFRS 7, IFRS 9, IFRS 17; IAS 1, IAS 32, IAS 36, IAS 38	
Classification of Liabilities as Current or Non-current—Deferral of Effective Date Amendment to IAS 1	July 2020	1 January 2023	IAS 1	
(a) Amendments to this Standard were issued in June 2020.				
(b) In July 2020, the effective date of this amendment was deferred to 1 January 2023.				

The summaries that follow explain the changes that will be introduced by the documents mentioned in the table *Standards issued, but not effective, at 1 January 2021.*

Sale or Contribution of Assets between an Investor and its Associate or Joint Venture

Sale or Contribution of Assets between an Investor and its Associate or Joint Venture, which amends IFRS 10 and IAS 28, was issued in September 2014. The amendments address the conflict between the requirements in IFRS 10 *Consolidated Financial Statements* and IAS 28 *Investments in Associates and Joint Ventures* when accounting for the sale or contribution of a subsidiary to a joint venture or associate (resulting in the loss of control of the subsidiary). In December 2015 the Board deferred the effective date of this amendment indefinitely.

IFRS 17 *Insurance Contracts* and *Amendments to IFRS 17*

IFRS 17 *Insurance Contracts* applies to: insurance contracts, including reinsurance contracts, issued by an entity with specified exceptions; reinsurance contracts held by an entity; and investment contracts with discretionary participation features issued by an entity that issues insurance contracts. An insurance contract is defined as 'a contract under which one party (the issuer) accepts significant insurance risk from another party (the policyholder) by agreeing to compensate the policyholder if a specified uncertain future event (the insured event) adversely affects the policyholder'.

In the statement of financial position, an entity is required to measure profitable insurance contracts at the risk-adjusted present value of the future cash flows plus unearned profit for services to be provided under the contract.

IFRS 17 requires an entity to recognise profit from a group of insurance contracts over the period the entity provides services, and as the entity is released from risk. If a group of contracts is or becomes loss-making, the entity is required to recognise the loss immediately.

The Standard also requires insurance revenue, insurance service expenses, and insurance finance income or expenses to be presented separately.

Since the Board issued IFRS 17 in May 2017, it has been carrying out activities to support entities and monitor their progress in implementing the Standard. These activities helped the Board to understand the concerns and challenges that some entities identified while implementing the Standard. The Board considered these concerns and challenges and decided to amend IFRS 17. The objective of the amendments is to assist entities implementing the Standard, while not unduly disrupting implementation or diminishing the usefulness of the information provided by applying IFRS 17.

IFRS 17, as amended in June 2020, is effective for annual reporting periods beginning on or after 1 January 2023.

Classification of Liabilities as Current and Non-current and Classification of Liabilities as Current and Non-current—Deferral of Effective Date

Classification of Liabilities as Current or Non-current clarifies a criterion in IAS 1 *Presentation of Financial Statements* for classifying a liability as non-current: the requirement for an entity to have the right to defer settlement of the liability for at least 12 months after the reporting period.

Classification of Liabilities as Current or Non-current—Deferral of Effective Date was issued in July 2020 and deferred the mandatory effective date of amendments to IAS 1 *Classification of Liabilities as Current or Non-current* to annual reporting periods beginning on or after 1 January 2023.

Reference to the Conceptual Framework

Reference to the Conceptual Framework updates a reference to the *Conceptual Framework* in IFRS 3 *Business Combinations* and makes further amendments to IFRS 3 to avoid unintended consequences of updating the reference.

Onerous Contracts—Cost of Fulfilling a Contract

Onerous Contracts—Cost of Fulfilling a Contract amends IAS 37 *Provisions, Contingent Liabilities and Contingent Assets*. The amendments clarify that for the purpose of assessing whether a contract is onerous, the cost of fulfilling the contract includes both the incremental costs of fulfilling that contract and an allocation of other costs that relate directly to fulfilling contracts.

Property, Plant and Equipment: Proceeds before Intended Use

Property, Plant and Equipment: Proceeds before Intended Use amends IAS 16 *Property, Plant and Equipment*. The amendments prohibit an entity from deducting from the cost of property, plant and equipment amounts received from selling items produced while the entity is preparing the asset for its intended use. Instead, an entity will recognise such sales proceeds and related cost in profit or loss.

Annual Improvements to IFRS Standards 2018-2020

Annual Improvements to IFRS Standards 2018-2020 contains the following amendments.

Standard	Subject of amendment
IFRS 1 *First-time Adoption of International Financial Reporting Standards*	Subsidiary as a First-time Adopter
IFRS 9 *Financial Instruments*	Fees in the '10 per cent' Test for Derecognition of Financial Liabilities
IAS 41 *Agriculture*	Taxation in Fair Value Measurements

Preface to IFRS® Standards

1   This Preface is issued to explain the scope, authority and timing of application of IFRS Standards. The Preface was most recently amended in December 2018.

2   The International Accounting Standards Board (Board) was established in 2001. The Board was preceded by the Board of the International Accounting Standards Committee (IASC). When the term IFRS Standards is used in this Preface, it includes Standards and IFRIC® Interpretations issued by the Board, and International Accounting Standards and SIC® Interpretations issued by its predecessor, the IASC.

3   The *Conceptual Framework for Financial Reporting* (*Conceptual Framework*) is not a Standard. The *Conceptual Framework* describes the objective of, and the concepts for, general purpose financial statements and other financial reporting. The purpose of the *Conceptual Framework* is to:

(a)   assist the Board to develop Standards that are based on consistent concepts;

(b)   assist preparers to develop consistent accounting policies when no Standard applies to a particular transaction or other event, or when a Standard allows a choice of accounting policies; and

(c)   assist all parties to understand and interpret the Standards.

4   IFRS Standards are developed through an international due process set out in the IFRS Foundation *Due Process Handbook*.

Scope and authority of IFRS Standards

5   The Standards are designed to apply to the general purpose financial statements and other financial reporting of profit-oriented entities.

6   The objective of general purpose financial statements is to provide financial information about the reporting entity that is useful to existing and potential investors, lenders and other creditors in making decisions relating to providing resources to the entity.

7   Other financial reporting comprises information provided outside financial statements that assists in the interpretation of a complete set of financial statements or improves users' ability to make efficient economic decisions.

8   Profit-oriented entities include those engaged in commercial, industrial, financial and similar activities, whether organised in corporate or in other forms. They include organisations such as mutual insurance companies and other mutual cooperative entities that provide dividends or other economic benefits directly and proportionately to their owners, members or participants.

9   Although IFRS Standards are not designed to apply to not-for-profit activities in the private sector, public sector or government, entities with such activities may find them appropriate. The International Public Sector Accounting Standards Board (IPSASB) prepares accounting standards for governments and

other public sector entities, other than government business entities, based on IFRS Standards.

10   The Standards set out recognition, measurement, presentation and disclosure requirements dealing with transactions and events that are important in general purpose financial statements. They may also set out such requirements for transactions and events that arise mainly in specific industries.

11   Some Standards permit different treatments for given transactions and events. The Board's objective is to require like transactions and events to be accounted for and reported in a like way and unlike transactions and events to be accounted for and reported differently, both within an entity over time and among entities. Consequently, the Board intends not to permit choices in accounting treatment. Also, the Board has reconsidered, and will continue to reconsider, those transactions and events for which Standards permit a choice of accounting treatment, with the objective of reducing the number of those choices.

Timing of application of IFRS Standards

12   IFRS Standards apply from a date specified in the document. New or revised Standards set out transitional provisions to be applied on their initial application. Exposure drafts are issued for comment and their proposals are subject to revision. Until the effective date of a Standard, the requirements of any Standard that would be affected by proposals in an exposure draft remain in force.

13   The Board has no general policy of exempting transactions occurring before a specific date from the requirements of new Standards. When financial statements are used to monitor compliance with contracts and agreements, a new Standard may have consequences that were not foreseen when the contract or agreement was finalised. For example, covenants contained in banking and loan agreements may impose limits on measures shown in a borrower's financial statements. The Board believes the fact that financial reporting requirements evolve and change over time is well understood and would be known to the parties when they entered into the agreement. It is up to the parties to determine whether the agreement should be insulated from the effects of a future Standard, or, if not, the manner in which the agreement might be renegotiated to reflect changes in reporting rather than changes in the underlying financial condition.

Format and language

14   Standards issued by the Board include paragraphs in bold type and plain type, which have equal authority. Paragraphs in bold type indicate the main principles. An individual Standard should be read in the context of the objective stated in that Standard.

15   The approved text of any discussion document, exposure draft or Standard is that approved by the Board in the English language. The Board may approve translations in other languages, provided that the translation is prepared in accordance with a process that provides assurance of the quality of the translation, and the Board may license other translations.

Conceptual Framework for Financial Reporting

Conceptual Framework for Financial Reporting was issued by the International Accounting Standards Board in September 2010. It was revised in March 2018.

CONTENTS

continued...

CHAPTER 5—RECOGNITION AND DERECOGNITION

CHAPTER 6—MEASUREMENT

CHAPTER 7—PRESENTATION AND DISCLOSURE

continued...

...continued

CHAPTER 8—CONCEPTS OF CAPITAL AND CAPITAL MAINTENANCE

FOR THE BASIS FOR CONCLUSIONS, SEE PART C OF THIS EDITION

BASIS FOR CONCLUSIONS

STATUS AND PURPOSE OF THE *CONCEPTUAL FRAMEWORK*

SP1.1   The *Conceptual Framework for Financial Reporting* (*Conceptual Framework*) describes the objective of, and the concepts for, general purpose financial reporting. The purpose of the *Conceptual Framework* is to:

(a)   assist the International Accounting Standards Board (Board) to develop IFRS Standards (Standards) that are based on consistent concepts;

(b)   assist preparers to develop consistent accounting policies when no Standard applies to a particular transaction or other event, or when a Standard allows a choice of accounting policy; and

(c)   assist all parties to understand and interpret the Standards.

SP1.2   The *Conceptual Framework* is not a Standard. Nothing in the *Conceptual Framework* overrides any Standard or any requirement in a Standard.

SP1.3   To meet the objective of general purpose financial reporting, the Board may sometimes specify requirements that depart from aspects of the *Conceptual Framework*. If the Board does so, it will explain the departure in the Basis for Conclusions on that Standard.

SP1.4   The *Conceptual Framework* may be revised from time to time on the basis of the Board's experience of working with it. Revisions of the *Conceptual Framework* will not automatically lead to changes to the Standards. Any decision to amend a Standard would require the Board to go through its due process for adding a project to its agenda and developing an amendment to that Standard.

SP1.5   The *Conceptual Framework* contributes to the stated mission of the IFRS Foundation and of the Board, which is part of the IFRS Foundation. That mission is to develop Standards that bring transparency, accountability and efficiency to financial markets around the world. The Board's work serves the public interest by fostering trust, growth and long-term financial stability in the global economy. The *Conceptual Framework* provides the foundation for Standards that:

(a)   contribute to transparency by enhancing the international comparability and quality of financial information, enabling investors and other market participants to make informed economic decisions.

(b)   strengthen accountability by reducing the information gap between the providers of capital and the people to whom they have entrusted their money. Standards based on the *Conceptual Framework* provide information needed to hold management to account. As a source of globally comparable information, those Standards are also of vital importance to regulators around the world.

(c)   contribute to economic efficiency by helping investors to identify opportunities and risks across the world, thus improving capital allocation. For businesses, the use of a single, trusted accounting language derived from Standards based on the *Conceptual Framework* lowers the cost of capital and reduces international reporting costs.

Contents

Introduction

1.1 The objective of general purpose financial reporting forms the foundation of the *Conceptual Framework*. Other aspects of the *Conceptual Framework* — the qualitative characteristics of, and the cost constraint on, useful financial information, a reporting entity concept, elements of financial statements, recognition and derecognition, measurement, presentation and disclosure — flow logically from the objective.

Objective, usefulness and limitations of general purpose financial reporting

1.2 The objective of general purpose financial reporting[1] is to provide financial information about the reporting entity that is useful to existing and potential investors, lenders and other creditors in making decisions relating to providing resources to the entity.[2] Those decisions involve decisions about:

    (a) buying, selling or holding equity and debt instruments;

    (b) providing or settling loans and other forms of credit; or

    (c) exercising rights to vote on, or otherwise influence, management's actions that affect the use of the entity's economic resources.

1.3 The decisions described in paragraph 1.2 depend on the returns that existing and potential investors, lenders and other creditors expect, for example, dividends, principal and interest payments or market price increases. Investors', lenders' and other creditors' expectations about returns depend on their assessment of the amount, timing and uncertainty of (the prospects for) future net cash inflows to the entity and on their assessment of management's stewardship of the entity's economic resources. Existing and potential investors, lenders and other creditors need information to help them make those assessments.

1.4 To make the assessments described in paragraph 1.3, existing and potential investors, lenders and other creditors need information about:

    (a) the economic resources of the entity, claims against the entity and changes in those resources and claims (see paragraphs 1.12–1.21); and

    (b) how efficiently and effectively the entity's management and governing board[3] have discharged their responsibilities to use the entity's economic resources (see paragraphs 1.22–1.23).

---

1 Throughout the *Conceptual Framework*, the terms 'financial reports' and 'financial reporting' refer to general purpose financial reports and general purpose financial reporting unless specifically indicated otherwise.

2 Throughout the *Conceptual Framework*, the term 'entity' refers to the reporting entity unless specifically indicated otherwise.

3 Throughout the *Conceptual Framework*, the term 'management' refers to management and the governing board of an entity unless specifically indicated otherwise.

1.5   Many existing and potential investors, lenders and other creditors cannot require reporting entities to provide information directly to them and must rely on general purpose financial reports for much of the financial information they need. Consequently, they are the primary users to whom general purpose financial reports are directed.[4]

1.6   However, general purpose financial reports do not and cannot provide all of the information that existing and potential investors, lenders and other creditors need. Those users need to consider pertinent information from other sources, for example, general economic conditions and expectations, political events and political climate, and industry and company outlooks.

1.7   General purpose financial reports are not designed to show the value of a reporting entity; but they provide information to help existing and potential investors, lenders and other creditors to estimate the value of the reporting entity.

1.8   Individual primary users have different, and possibly conflicting, information needs and desires. The Board, in developing Standards, will seek to provide the information set that will meet the needs of the maximum number of primary users. However, focusing on common information needs does not prevent the reporting entity from including additional information that is most useful to a particular subset of primary users.

1.9   The management of a reporting entity is also interested in financial information about the entity. However, management need not rely on general purpose financial reports because it is able to obtain the financial information it needs internally.

1.10   Other parties, such as regulators and members of the public other than investors, lenders and other creditors, may also find general purpose financial reports useful. However, those reports are not primarily directed to these other groups.

1.11   To a large extent, financial reports are based on estimates, judgements and models rather than exact depictions. The *Conceptual Framework* establishes the concepts that underlie those estimates, judgements and models. The concepts are the goal towards which the Board and preparers of financial reports strive. As with most goals, the *Conceptual Framework*'s vision of ideal financial reporting is unlikely to be achieved in full, at least not in the short term, because it takes time to understand, accept and implement new ways of analysing transactions and other events. Nevertheless, establishing a goal towards which to strive is essential if financial reporting is to evolve so as to improve its usefulness.

---

4   Throughout the *Conceptual Framework*, the terms 'primary users' and 'users' refer to those existing and potential investors, lenders and other creditors who must rely on general purpose financial reports for much of the financial information they need.

     © IFRS Foundation

Information about a reporting entity's economic resources, claims against the entity and changes in resources and claims

1.12   General purpose financial reports provide information about the financial position of a reporting entity, which is information about the entity's economic resources and the claims against the reporting entity. Financial reports also provide information about the effects of transactions and other events that change a reporting entity's economic resources and claims. Both types of information provide useful input for decisions relating to providing resources to an entity.

Economic resources and claims

1.13   Information about the nature and amounts of a reporting entity's economic resources and claims can help users to identify the reporting entity's financial strengths and weaknesses. That information can help users to assess the reporting entity's liquidity and solvency, its needs for additional financing and how successful it is likely to be in obtaining that financing. That information can also help users to assess management's stewardship of the entity's economic resources. Information about priorities and payment requirements of existing claims helps users to predict how future cash flows will be distributed among those with a claim against the reporting entity.

1.14   Different types of economic resources affect a user's assessment of the reporting entity's prospects for future cash flows differently. Some future cash flows result directly from existing economic resources, such as accounts receivable. Other cash flows result from using several resources in combination to produce and market goods or services to customers. Although those cash flows cannot be identified with individual economic resources (or claims), users of financial reports need to know the nature and amount of the resources available for use in a reporting entity's operations.

Changes in economic resources and claims

1.15   Changes in a reporting entity's economic resources and claims result from that entity's financial performance (see paragraphs 1.17–1.20) and from other events or transactions such as issuing debt or equity instruments (see paragraph 1.21). To properly assess both the prospects for future net cash inflows to the reporting entity and management's stewardship of the entity's economic resources, users need to be able to identify those two types of changes.

1.16   Information about a reporting entity's financial performance helps users to understand the return that the entity has produced on its economic resources. Information about the return the entity has produced can help users to assess management's stewardship of the entity's economic resources. Information about the variability and components of that return is also important, especially in assessing the uncertainty of future cash flows. Information about a reporting entity's past financial performance and how its management discharged its stewardship responsibilities is usually helpful in predicting the entity's future returns on its economic resources.

Financial performance reflected by accrual accounting

1.17 Accrual accounting depicts the effects of transactions and other events and circumstances on a reporting entity's economic resources and claims in the periods in which those effects occur, even if the resulting cash receipts and payments occur in a different period. This is important because information about a reporting entity's economic resources and claims and changes in its economic resources and claims during a period provides a better basis for assessing the entity's past and future performance than information solely about cash receipts and payments during that period.

1.18 Information about a reporting entity's financial performance during a period, reflected by changes in its economic resources and claims other than by obtaining additional resources directly from investors and creditors (see paragraph 1.21), is useful in assessing the entity's past and future ability to generate net cash inflows. That information indicates the extent to which the reporting entity has increased its available economic resources, and thus its capacity for generating net cash inflows through its operations rather than by obtaining additional resources directly from investors and creditors. Information about a reporting entity's financial performance during a period can also help users to assess management's stewardship of the entity's economic resources.

1.19 Information about a reporting entity's financial performance during a period may also indicate the extent to which events such as changes in market prices or interest rates have increased or decreased the entity's economic resources and claims, thereby affecting the entity's ability to generate net cash inflows.

Financial performance reflected by past cash flows

1.20 Information about a reporting entity's cash flows during a period also helps users to assess the entity's ability to generate future net cash inflows and to assess management's stewardship of the entity's economic resources. That information indicates how the reporting entity obtains and spends cash, including information about its borrowing and repayment of debt, cash dividends or other cash distributions to investors, and other factors that may affect the entity's liquidity or solvency. Information about cash flows helps users understand a reporting entity's operations, evaluate its financing and investing activities, assess its liquidity or solvency and interpret other information about financial performance.

Changes in economic resources and claims not resulting from financial performance

1.21 A reporting entity's economic resources and claims may also change for reasons other than financial performance, such as issuing debt or equity instruments. Information about this type of change is necessary to give users a complete understanding of why the reporting entity's economic resources and claims changed and the implications of those changes for its future financial performance.

Information about use of the entity's economic resources

1.22   Information about how efficiently and effectively the reporting entity's management has discharged its responsibilities to use the entity's economic resources helps users to assess management's stewardship of those resources. Such information is also useful for predicting how efficiently and effectively management will use the entity's economic resources in future periods. Hence, it can be useful for assessing the entity's prospects for future net cash inflows.

1.23   Examples of management's responsibilities to use the entity's economic resources include protecting those resources from unfavourable effects of economic factors, such as price and technological changes, and ensuring that the entity complies with applicable laws, regulations and contractual provisions.

CONTENTS

Introduction

2.1   The qualitative characteristics of useful financial information discussed in this chapter identify the types of information that are likely to be most useful to the existing and potential investors, lenders and other creditors for making decisions about the reporting entity on the basis of information in its financial report (financial information).

2.2   Financial reports provide information about the reporting entity's economic resources, claims against the reporting entity and the effects of transactions and other events and conditions that change those resources and claims. (This information is referred to in the *Conceptual Framework* as information about the economic phenomena.) Some financial reports also include explanatory material about management's expectations and strategies for the reporting entity, and other types of forward-looking information.

2.3   The qualitative characteristics of useful financial information[5] apply to financial information provided in financial statements, as well as to financial information provided in other ways. Cost, which is a pervasive constraint on the reporting entity's ability to provide useful financial information, applies similarly. However, the considerations in applying the qualitative characteristics and the cost constraint may be different for different types of information. For example, applying them to forward-looking information may be different from applying them to information about existing economic resources and claims and to changes in those resources and claims.

Qualitative characteristics of useful financial information

2.4   If financial information is to be useful, it must be relevant and faithfully represent what it purports to represent. The usefulness of financial information is enhanced if it is comparable, verifiable, timely and understandable.

Fundamental qualitative characteristics

2.5   The fundamental qualitative characteristics are relevance and faithful representation.

Relevance

2.6   Relevant financial information is capable of making a difference in the decisions made by users. Information may be capable of making a difference in a decision even if some users choose not to take advantage of it or are already aware of it from other sources.

2.7   Financial information is capable of making a difference in decisions if it has predictive value, confirmatory value or both.

---

5   Throughout the *Conceptual Framework*, the terms 'qualitative characteristics' and 'cost constraint' refer to the qualitative characteristics of, and the cost constraint on, useful financial information.

2.8   Financial information has predictive value if it can be used as an input to processes employed by users to predict future outcomes. Financial information need not be a prediction or forecast to have predictive value. Financial information with predictive value is employed by users in making their own predictions.

2.9   Financial information has confirmatory value if it provides feedback about (confirms or changes) previous evaluations.

2.10   The predictive value and confirmatory value of financial information are interrelated. Information that has predictive value often also has confirmatory value. For example, revenue information for the current year, which can be used as the basis for predicting revenues in future years, can also be compared with revenue predictions for the current year that were made in past years. The results of those comparisons can help a user to correct and improve the processes that were used to make those previous predictions.

Materiality

2.11   Information is material if omitting, misstating or obscuring it could reasonably be expected to influence decisions that the primary users of general purpose financial reports (see paragraph 1.5) make on the basis of those reports, which provide financial information about a specific reporting entity. In other words, materiality is an entity-specific aspect of relevance based on the nature or magnitude, or both, of the items to which the information relates in the context of an individual entity's financial report. Consequently, the Board cannot specify a uniform quantitative threshold for materiality or predetermine what could be material in a particular situation.

Faithful representation

2.12   Financial reports represent economic phenomena in words and numbers. To be useful, financial information must not only represent relevant phenomena, but it must also faithfully represent the substance of the phenomena that it purports to represent. In many circumstances, the substance of an economic phenomenon and its legal form are the same. If they are not the same, providing information only about the legal form would not faithfully represent the economic phenomenon (see paragraphs 4.59–4.62).

2.13   To be a perfectly faithful representation, a depiction would have three characteristics. It would be complete, neutral and free from error. Of course, perfection is seldom, if ever, achievable. The Board's objective is to maximise those qualities to the extent possible.

2.14   A complete depiction includes all information necessary for a user to understand the phenomenon being depicted, including all necessary descriptions and explanations. For example, a complete depiction of a group of assets would include, at a minimum, a description of the nature of the assets in the group, a numerical depiction of all of the assets in the group, and a description of what the numerical depiction represents (for example, historical cost or fair value). For some items, a complete depiction may also entail explanations of significant facts about the quality and nature of the items, factors and circumstances that might affect their quality and nature, and the process used to determine the numerical depiction.

2.15   A neutral depiction is without bias in the selection or presentation of financial information. A neutral depiction is not slanted, weighted, emphasised, de-emphasised or otherwise manipulated to increase the probability that financial information will be received favourably or unfavourably by users. Neutral information does not mean information with no purpose or no influence on behaviour. On the contrary, relevant financial information is, by definition, capable of making a difference in users' decisions.

2.16   Neutrality is supported by the exercise of prudence. Prudence is the exercise of caution when making judgements under conditions of uncertainty. The exercise of prudence means that assets and income are not overstated and liabilities and expenses are not understated.[6] Equally, the exercise of prudence does not allow for the understatement of assets or income or the overstatement of liabilities or expenses. Such misstatements can lead to the overstatement or understatement of income or expenses in future periods.

2.17   The exercise of prudence does not imply a need for asymmetry, for example, a systematic need for more persuasive evidence to support the recognition of assets or income than the recognition of liabilities or expenses. Such asymmetry is not a qualitative characteristic of useful financial information. Nevertheless, particular Standards may contain asymmetric requirements if this is a consequence of decisions intended to select the most relevant information that faithfully represents what it purports to represent.

2.18   Faithful representation does not mean accurate in all respects. Free from error means there are no errors or omissions in the description of the phenomenon, and the process used to produce the reported information has been selected and applied with no errors in the process. In this context, free from error does not mean perfectly accurate in all respects. For example, an estimate of an unobservable price or value cannot be determined to be accurate or inaccurate. However, a representation of that estimate can be faithful if the amount is described clearly and accurately as being an estimate, the nature and limitations of the estimating process are explained, and no errors have been made in selecting and applying an appropriate process for developing the estimate.

2.19   When monetary amounts in financial reports cannot be observed directly and must instead be estimated, measurement uncertainty arises. The use of reasonable estimates is an essential part of the preparation of financial information and does not undermine the usefulness of the information if the estimates are clearly and accurately described and explained. Even a high level of measurement uncertainty does not necessarily prevent such an estimate from providing useful information (see paragraph 2.22).

---

6   Assets, liabilities, income and expenses are defined in Table 4.1. They are the elements of financial statements.

Applying the fundamental qualitative characteristics

2.20   Information must both be relevant and provide a faithful representation of what it purports to represent if it is to be useful. Neither a faithful representation of an irrelevant phenomenon nor an unfaithful representation of a relevant phenomenon helps users make good decisions.

2.21   The most efficient and effective process for applying the fundamental qualitative characteristics would usually be as follows (subject to the effects of enhancing characteristics and the cost constraint, which are not considered in this example). First, identify an economic phenomenon, information about which is capable of being useful to users of the reporting entity's financial information. Second, identify the type of information about that phenomenon that would be most relevant. Third, determine whether that information is available and whether it can provide a faithful representation of the economic phenomenon. If so, the process of satisfying the fundamental qualitative characteristics ends at that point. If not, the process is repeated with the next most relevant type of information.

2.22   In some cases, a trade-off between the fundamental qualitative characteristics may need to be made in order to meet the objective of financial reporting, which is to provide useful information about economic phenomena. For example, the most relevant information about a phenomenon may be a highly uncertain estimate. In some cases, the level of measurement uncertainty involved in making that estimate may be so high that it may be questionable whether the estimate would provide a sufficiently faithful representation of that phenomenon. In some such cases, the most useful information may be the highly uncertain estimate, accompanied by a description of the estimate and an explanation of the uncertainties that affect it. In other such cases, if that information would not provide a sufficiently faithful representation of that phenomenon, the most useful information may include an estimate of another type that is slightly less relevant but is subject to lower measurement uncertainty. In limited circumstances, there may be no estimate that provides useful information. In those limited circumstances, it may be necessary to provide information that does not rely on an estimate.

Enhancing qualitative characteristics

2.23   Comparability, verifiability, timeliness and understandability are qualitative characteristics that enhance the usefulness of information that both is relevant and provides a faithful representation of what it purports to represent. The enhancing qualitative characteristics may also help determine which of two ways should be used to depict a phenomenon if both are considered to provide equally relevant information and an equally faithful representation of that phenomenon.

Comparability

2.24 Users' decisions involve choosing between alternatives, for example, selling or holding an investment, or investing in one reporting entity or another. Consequently, information about a reporting entity is more useful if it can be compared with similar information about other entities and with similar information about the same entity for another period or another date.

2.25 Comparability is the qualitative characteristic that enables users to identify and understand similarities in, and differences among, items. Unlike the other qualitative characteristics, comparability does not relate to a single item. A comparison requires at least two items.

2.26 Consistency, although related to comparability, is not the same. Consistency refers to the use of the same methods for the same items, either from period to period within a reporting entity or in a single period across entities. Comparability is the goal; consistency helps to achieve that goal.

2.27 Comparability is not uniformity. For information to be comparable, like things must look alike and different things must look different. Comparability of financial information is not enhanced by making unlike things look alike any more than it is enhanced by making like things look different.

2.28 Some degree of comparability is likely to be attained by satisfying the fundamental qualitative characteristics. A faithful representation of a relevant economic phenomenon should naturally possess some degree of comparability with a faithful representation of a similar relevant economic phenomenon by another reporting entity.

2.29 Although a single economic phenomenon can be faithfully represented in multiple ways, permitting alternative accounting methods for the same economic phenomenon diminishes comparability.

Verifiability

2.30 Verifiability helps assure users that information faithfully represents the economic phenomena it purports to represent. Verifiability means that different knowledgeable and independent observers could reach consensus, although not necessarily complete agreement, that a particular depiction is a faithful representation. Quantified information need not be a single point estimate to be verifiable. A range of possible amounts and the related probabilities can also be verified.

2.31 Verification can be direct or indirect. Direct verification means verifying an amount or other representation through direct observation, for example, by counting cash. Indirect verification means checking the inputs to a model, formula or other technique and recalculating the outputs using the same methodology. An example is verifying the carrying amount of inventory by checking the inputs (quantities and costs) and recalculating the ending inventory using the same cost flow assumption (for example, using the first-in, first-out method).

2.32   It may not be possible to verify some explanations and forward-looking financial information until a future period, if at all. To help users decide whether they want to use that information, it would normally be necessary to disclose the underlying assumptions, the methods of compiling the information and other factors and circumstances that support the information.

Timeliness

2.33   Timeliness means having information available to decision-makers in time to be capable of influencing their decisions. Generally, the older the information is the less useful it is. However, some information may continue to be timely long after the end of a reporting period because, for example, some users may need to identify and assess trends.

Understandability

2.34   Classifying, characterising and presenting information clearly and concisely makes it understandable.

2.35   Some phenomena are inherently complex and cannot be made easy to understand. Excluding information about those phenomena from financial reports might make the information in those financial reports easier to understand. However, those reports would be incomplete and therefore possibly misleading.

2.36   Financial reports are prepared for users who have a reasonable knowledge of business and economic activities and who review and analyse the information diligently. At times, even well-informed and diligent users may need to seek the aid of an adviser to understand information about complex economic phenomena.

Applying the enhancing qualitative characteristics

2.37   Enhancing qualitative characteristics should be maximised to the extent possible. However, the enhancing qualitative characteristics, either individually or as a group, cannot make information useful if that information is irrelevant or does not provide a faithful representation of what it purports to represent.

2.38   Applying the enhancing qualitative characteristics is an iterative process that does not follow a prescribed order. Sometimes, one enhancing qualitative characteristic may have to be diminished to maximise another qualitative characteristic. For example, a temporary reduction in comparability as a result of prospectively applying a new Standard may be worthwhile to improve relevance or faithful representation in the longer term. Appropriate disclosures may partially compensate for non-comparability.

The cost constraint on useful financial reporting

2.39   Cost is a pervasive constraint on the information that can be provided by financial reporting. Reporting financial information imposes costs, and it is important that those costs are justified by the benefits of reporting that information. There are several types of costs and benefits to consider.

2.40   Providers of financial information expend most of the effort involved in collecting, processing, verifying and disseminating financial information, but users ultimately bear those costs in the form of reduced returns. Users of financial information also incur costs of analysing and interpreting the information provided. If needed information is not provided, users incur additional costs to obtain that information elsewhere or to estimate it.

2.41   Reporting financial information that is relevant and faithfully represents what it purports to represent helps users to make decisions with more confidence. This results in more efficient functioning of capital markets and a lower cost of capital for the economy as a whole. An individual investor, lender or other creditor also receives benefits by making more informed decisions. However, it is not possible for general purpose financial reports to provide all the information that every user finds relevant.

2.42   In applying the cost constraint, the Board assesses whether the benefits of reporting particular information are likely to justify the costs incurred to provide and use that information. When applying the cost constraint in developing a proposed Standard, the Board seeks information from providers of financial information, users, auditors, academics and others about the expected nature and quantity of the benefits and costs of that Standard. In most situations, assessments are based on a combination of quantitative and qualitative information.

2.43   Because of the inherent subjectivity, different individuals' assessments of the costs and benefits of reporting particular items of financial information will vary. Therefore, the Board seeks to consider costs and benefits in relation to financial reporting generally, and not just in relation to individual reporting entities. That does not mean that assessments of costs and benefits always justify the same reporting requirements for all entities. Differences may be appropriate because of different sizes of entities, different ways of raising capital (publicly or privately), different users' needs or other factors.

Conceptual Framework

CONTENTS

Financial statements

3.1   Chapters 1 and 2 discuss information provided in general purpose financial reports and Chapters 3–8 discuss information provided in general purpose financial statements, which are a particular form of general purpose financial reports. Financial statements[7] provide information about economic resources of the reporting entity, claims against the entity, and changes in those resources and claims, that meet the definitions of the elements of financial statements (see Table 4.1).

Objective and scope of financial statements

3.2   The objective of financial statements is to provide financial information about the reporting entity's assets, liabilities, equity, income and expenses[8] that is useful to users of financial statements in assessing the prospects for future net cash inflows to the reporting entity and in assessing management's stewardship of the entity's economic resources (see paragraph 1.3).

3.3   That information is provided:

(a)   in the statement of financial position, by recognising assets, liabilities and equity;

(b)   in the statement(s) of financial performance,[9] by recognising income and expenses; and

(c)   in other statements and notes, by presenting and disclosing information about:

(i)   recognised assets, liabilities, equity, income and expenses (see paragraph 5.1), including information about their nature and about the risks arising from those recognised assets and liabilities;

(ii)   assets and liabilities that have not been recognised (see paragraph 5.6), including information about their nature and about the risks arising from them;

(iii)   cash flows;

(iv)   contributions from holders of equity claims and distributions to them; and

(v)   the methods, assumptions and judgements used in estimating the amounts presented or disclosed, and changes in those methods, assumptions and judgements.

---

7   Throughout the *Conceptual Framework*, the term 'financial statements' refers to general purpose financial statements.

8   Assets, liabilities, equity, income and expenses are defined in Table 4.1. They are the elements of financial statements.

9   The *Conceptual Framework* does not specify whether the statement(s) of financial performance comprise(s) a single statement or two statements.

Reporting period

3.4   Financial statements are prepared for a specified period of time (reporting period) and provide information about:

(a)   assets and liabilities – including unrecognised assets and liabilities – and equity that existed at the end of the reporting period, or during the reporting period; and

(b)   income and expenses for the reporting period.

3.5   To help users of financial statements to identify and assess changes and trends, financial statements also provide comparative information for at least one preceding reporting period.

3.6   Information about possible future transactions and other possible future events (forward-looking information) is included in financial statements if it:

(a)   relates to the entity's assets or liabilities – including unrecognised assets or liabilities – or equity that existed at the end of the reporting period, or during the reporting period, or to income or expenses for the reporting period; and

(b)   is useful to users of financial statements.

For example, if an asset or liability is measured by estimating future cash flows, information about those estimated future cash flows may help users of financial statements to understand the reported measures. Financial statements do not typically provide other types of forward-looking information, for example, explanatory material about management's expectations and strategies for the reporting entity.

3.7   Financial statements include information about transactions and other events that have occurred after the end of the reporting period if providing that information is necessary to meet the objective of financial statements (see paragraph 3.2).

Perspective adopted in financial statements

3.8   Financial statements provide information about transactions and other events viewed from the perspective of the reporting entity as a whole, not from the perspective of any particular group of the entity's existing or potential investors, lenders or other creditors.

Going concern assumption

3.9   Financial statements are normally prepared on the assumption that the reporting entity is a going concern and will continue in operation for the foreseeable future. Hence, it is assumed that the entity has neither the intention nor the need to enter liquidation or to cease trading. If such an intention or need exists, the financial statements may have to be prepared on a different basis. If so, the financial statements describe the basis used.

The reporting entity

3.10   A reporting entity is an entity that is required, or chooses, to prepare financial statements. A reporting entity can be a single entity or a portion of an entity or can comprise more than one entity. A reporting entity is not necessarily a legal entity.

3.11   Sometimes one entity (parent) has control over another entity (subsidiary). If a reporting entity comprises both the parent and its subsidiaries, the reporting entity's financial statements are referred to as 'consolidated financial statements' (see paragraphs 3.15–3.16). If a reporting entity is the parent alone, the reporting entity's financial statements are referred to as 'unconsolidated financial statements' (see paragraphs 3.17–3.18).

3.12   If a reporting entity comprises two or more entities that are not all linked by a parent-subsidiary relationship, the reporting entity's financial statements are referred to as 'combined financial statements'.

3.13   Determining the appropriate boundary of a reporting entity can be difficult if the reporting entity:

   (a)   is not a legal entity; and

   (b)   does not comprise only legal entities linked by a parent-subsidiary relationship.

3.14   In such cases, determining the boundary of the reporting entity is driven by the information needs of the primary users of the reporting entity's financial statements. Those users need relevant information that faithfully represents what it purports to represent. Faithful representation requires that:

   (a)   the boundary of the reporting entity does not contain an arbitrary or incomplete set of economic activities;

   (b)   including that set of economic activities within the boundary of the reporting entity results in neutral information; and

   (c)   a description is provided of how the boundary of the reporting entity was determined and of what constitutes the reporting entity.

Consolidated and unconsolidated financial statements

3.15   Consolidated financial statements provide information about the assets, liabilities, equity, income and expenses of both the parent and its subsidiaries as a single reporting entity. That information is useful for existing and potential investors, lenders and other creditors of the parent in their assessment of the prospects for future net cash inflows to the parent. This is because net cash inflows to the parent include distributions to the parent from its subsidiaries, and those distributions depend on net cash inflows to the subsidiaries.

3.16   Consolidated financial statements are not designed to provide separate information about the assets, liabilities, equity, income and expenses of any particular subsidiary. A subsidiary's own financial statements are designed to provide that information.

3.17   Unconsolidated financial statements are designed to provide information about the parent's assets, liabilities, equity, income and expenses, and not about those of its subsidiaries. That information can be useful to existing and potential investors, lenders and other creditors of the parent because:

(a)   a claim against the parent typically does not give the holder of that claim a claim against subsidiaries; and

(b)   in some jurisdictions, the amounts that can be legally distributed to holders of equity claims against the parent depend on the distributable reserves of the parent.

Another way to provide information about some or all assets, liabilities, equity, income and expenses of the parent alone is in consolidated financial statements, in the notes.

3.18   Information provided in unconsolidated financial statements is typically not sufficient to meet the information needs of existing and potential investors, lenders and other creditors of the parent. Accordingly, when consolidated financial statements are required, unconsolidated financial statements cannot serve as a substitute for consolidated financial statements. Nevertheless, a parent may be required, or choose, to prepare unconsolidated financial statements in addition to consolidated financial statements.

CONTENTS

Introduction

4.1   The elements of financial statements defined in the *Conceptual Framework* are:

(a)   assets, liabilities and equity, which relate to a reporting entity's financial position; and

(b)   income and expenses, which relate to a reporting entity's financial performance.

4.2   Those elements are linked to the economic resources, claims and changes in economic resources and claims discussed in Chapter 1, and are defined in Table 4.1.

Table 4.1 – The elements of financial statements

Item discussed in Chapter 1	Element	Definition or description
Economic resource	Asset	A present economic resource controlled by the entity as a result of past events. An economic resource is a right that has the potential to produce economic benefits.
Claim	Liability	A present obligation of the entity to transfer an economic resource as a result of past events.
	Equity	The residual interest in the assets of the entity after deducting all its liabilities.
Changes in economic resources and claims, reflecting financial performance	Income	Increases in assets, or decreases in liabilities, that result in increases in equity, other than those relating to contributions from holders of equity claims.
	Expenses	Decreases in assets, or increases in liabilities, that result in decreases in equity, other than those relating to distributions to holders of equity claims.
Other changes in economic resources and claims	–	Contributions from holders of equity claims, and distributions to them.
	–	Exchanges of assets or liabilities that do not result in increases or decreases in equity.

Definition of an asset

4.3   An asset is a present economic resource controlled by the entity as a result of past events.

4.4   An economic resource is a right that has the potential to produce economic benefits.

4.5   This section discusses three aspects of those definitions:

(a)   right (see paragraphs 4.6–4.13);

(b)   potential to produce economic benefits (see paragraphs 4.14–4.18); and

(c)   control (see paragraphs 4.19–4.25).

Right

4.6   Rights that have the potential to produce economic benefits take many forms, including:

    (a)   rights that correspond to an obligation of another party (see paragraph 4.39), for example:

        (i)   rights to receive cash.

        (ii)   rights to receive goods or services.

        (iii)   rights to exchange economic resources with another party on favourable terms. Such rights include, for example, a forward contract to buy an economic resource on terms that are currently favourable or an option to buy an economic resource.

        (iv)   rights to benefit from an obligation of another party to transfer an economic resource if a specified uncertain future event occurs (see paragraph 4.37).

    (b)   rights that do not correspond to an obligation of another party, for example:

        (i)   rights over physical objects, such as property, plant and equipment or inventories. Examples of such rights are a right to use a physical object or a right to benefit from the residual value of a leased object.

        (ii)   rights to use intellectual property.

4.7   Many rights are established by contract, legislation or similar means. For example, an entity might obtain rights from owning or leasing a physical object, from owning a debt instrument or an equity instrument, or from owning a registered patent. However, an entity might also obtain rights in other ways, for example:

    (a)   by acquiring or creating know-how that is not in the public domain (see paragraph 4.22); or

    (b)   through an obligation of another party that arises because that other party has no practical ability to act in a manner inconsistent with its customary practices, published policies or specific statements (see paragraph 4.31).

4.8   Some goods or services — for example, employee services — are received and immediately consumed. An entity's right to obtain the economic benefits produced by such goods or services exists momentarily until the entity consumes the goods or services.

4.9   Not all of an entity's rights are assets of that entity — to be assets of the entity, the rights must both have the potential to produce for the entity economic benefits beyond the economic benefits available to all other parties (see paragraphs 4.14–4.18) and be controlled by the entity (see paragraphs

4.19–4.25). For example, rights available to all parties without significant cost – for instance, rights of access to public goods, such as public rights of way over land, or know-how that is in the public domain – are typically not assets for the entities that hold them.

4.10   An entity cannot have a right to obtain economic benefits from itself. Hence:

(a)   debt instruments or equity instruments issued by the entity and repurchased and held by it – for example, treasury shares – are not economic resources of that entity; and

(b)   if a reporting entity comprises more than one legal entity, debt instruments or equity instruments issued by one of those legal entities and held by another of those legal entities are not economic resources of the reporting entity.

4.11   In principle, each of an entity's rights is a separate asset. However, for accounting purposes, related rights are often treated as a single unit of account that is a single asset (see paragraphs 4.48–4.55). For example, legal ownership of a physical object may give rise to several rights, including:

(a)   the right to use the object;

(b)   the right to sell rights over the object;

(c)   the right to pledge rights over the object; and

(d)   other rights not listed in (a)–(c).

4.12   In many cases, the set of rights arising from legal ownership of a physical object is accounted for as a single asset. Conceptually, the economic resource is the set of rights, not the physical object. Nevertheless, describing the set of rights as the physical object will often provide a faithful representation of those rights in the most concise and understandable way.

4.13   In some cases, it is uncertain whether a right exists. For example, an entity and another party might dispute whether the entity has a right to receive an economic resource from that other party. Until that existence uncertainty is resolved – for example, by a court ruling – it is uncertain whether the entity has a right and, consequently, whether an asset exists. (Paragraph 5.14 discusses recognition of assets whose existence is uncertain.)

Potential to produce economic benefits

4.14   An economic resource is a right that has the potential to produce economic benefits. For that potential to exist, it does not need to be certain, or even likely, that the right will produce economic benefits. It is only necessary that the right already exists and that, in at least one circumstance, it would produce for the entity economic benefits beyond those available to all other parties.

4.15   A right can meet the definition of an economic resource, and hence can be an asset, even if the probability that it will produce economic benefits is low. Nevertheless, that low probability might affect decisions about what information to provide about the asset and how to provide that information, including decisions about whether the asset is recognised (see paragraphs 5.15–5.17) and how it is measured.

4.16   An economic resource could produce economic benefits for an entity by entitling or enabling it to do, for example, one or more of the following:

(a)   receive contractual cash flows or another economic resource;

(b)   exchange economic resources with another party on favourable terms;

(c)   produce cash inflows or avoid cash outflows by, for example:

(i)   using the economic resource either individually or in combination with other economic resources to produce goods or provide services;

(ii)   using the economic resource to enhance the value of other economic resources; or

(iii)   leasing the economic resource to another party;

(d)   receive cash or other economic resources by selling the economic resource; or

(e)   extinguish liabilities by transferring the economic resource.

4.17   Although an economic resource derives its value from its present potential to produce future economic benefits, the economic resource is the present right that contains that potential, not the future economic benefits that the right may produce. For example, a purchased option derives its value from its potential to produce economic benefits through exercise of the option at a future date. However, the economic resource is the present right—the right to exercise the option at a future date. The economic resource is not the future economic benefits that the holder will receive if the option is exercised.

4.18   There is a close association between incurring expenditure and acquiring assets, but the two do not necessarily coincide. Hence, when an entity incurs expenditure, this may provide evidence that the entity has sought future economic benefits, but does not provide conclusive proof that the entity has obtained an asset. Similarly, the absence of related expenditure does not preclude an item from meeting the definition of an asset. Assets can include, for example, rights that a government has granted to the entity free of charge or that another party has donated to the entity.

Control

4.19   Control links an economic resource to an entity. Assessing whether control exists helps to identify the economic resource for which the entity accounts. For example, an entity may control a proportionate share in a property without controlling the rights arising from ownership of the entire property. In such cases, the entity's asset is the share in the property, which it controls, not the rights arising from ownership of the entire property, which it does not control.

4.20　　An entity controls an economic resource if it has the present ability to direct the use of the economic resource and obtain the economic benefits that may flow from it. Control includes the present ability to prevent other parties from directing the use of the economic resource and from obtaining the economic benefits that may flow from it. It follows that, if one party controls an economic resource, no other party controls that resource.

4.21　　An entity has the present ability to direct the use of an economic resource if it has the right to deploy that economic resource in its activities, or to allow another party to deploy the economic resource in that other party's activities.

4.22　　Control of an economic resource usually arises from an ability to enforce legal rights. However, control can also arise if an entity has other means of ensuring that it, and no other party, has the present ability to direct the use of the economic resource and obtain the benefits that may flow from it. For example, an entity could control a right to use know-how that is not in the public domain if the entity has access to the know-how and the present ability to keep the know-how secret, even if that know-how is not protected by a registered patent.

4.23　　For an entity to control an economic resource, the future economic benefits from that resource must flow to the entity either directly or indirectly rather than to another party. This aspect of control does not imply that the entity can ensure that the resource will produce economic benefits in all circumstances. Instead, it means that if the resource produces economic benefits, the entity is the party that will obtain them either directly or indirectly.

4.24　　Having exposure to significant variations in the amount of the economic benefits produced by an economic resource may indicate that the entity controls the resource. However, it is only one factor to consider in the overall assessment of whether control exists.

4.25　　Sometimes one party (a principal) engages another party (an agent) to act on behalf of, and for the benefit of, the principal. For example, a principal may engage an agent to arrange sales of goods controlled by the principal. If an agent has custody of an economic resource controlled by the principal, that economic resource is not an asset of the agent. Furthermore, if the agent has an obligation to transfer to a third party an economic resource controlled by the principal, that obligation is not a liability of the agent, because the economic resource that would be transferred is the principal's economic resource, not the agent's.

Definition of a liability

4.26　　A liability is a present obligation of the entity to transfer an economic resource as a result of past events.

4.27　　For a liability to exist, three criteria must all be satisfied:

　　　　(a)　　the entity has an obligation (see paragraphs 4.28–4.35);

(b)   the obligation is to transfer an economic resource (see paragraphs 4.36–4.41); and

(c)   the obligation is a present obligation that exists as a result of past events (see paragraphs 4.42–4.47).

Obligation

4.28   The first criterion for a liability is that the entity has an obligation.

4.29   An obligation is a duty or responsibility that an entity has no practical ability to avoid. An obligation is always owed to another party (or parties). The other party (or parties) could be a person or another entity, a group of people or other entities, or society at large. It is not necessary to know the identity of the party (or parties) to whom the obligation is owed.

4.30   If one party has an obligation to transfer an economic resource, it follows that another party (or parties) has a right to receive that economic resource. However, a requirement for one party to recognise a liability and measure it at a specified amount does not imply that the other party (or parties) must recognise an asset or measure it at the same amount. For example, particular Standards may contain different recognition criteria or measurement requirements for the liability of one party and the corresponding asset of the other party (or parties) if those different criteria or requirements are a consequence of decisions intended to select the most relevant information that faithfully represents what it purports to represent.

4.31   Many obligations are established by contract, legislation or similar means and are legally enforceable by the party (or parties) to whom they are owed. Obligations can also arise, however, from an entity's customary practices, published policies or specific statements if the entity has no practical ability to act in a manner inconsistent with those practices, policies or statements. The obligation that arises in such situations is sometimes referred to as a 'constructive obligation'.

4.32   In some situations, an entity's duty or responsibility to transfer an economic resource is conditional on a particular future action that the entity itself may take. Such actions could include operating a particular business or operating in a particular market on a specified future date, or exercising particular options within a contract. In such situations, the entity has an obligation if it has no practical ability to avoid taking that action.

4.33   A conclusion that it is appropriate to prepare an entity's financial statements on a going concern basis also implies a conclusion that the entity has no practical ability to avoid a transfer that could be avoided only by liquidating the entity or by ceasing to trade.

4.34   The factors used to assess whether an entity has the practical ability to avoid transferring an economic resource may depend on the nature of the entity's duty or responsibility. For example, in some cases, an entity may have no practical ability to avoid a transfer if any action that it could take to avoid the transfer would have economic consequences significantly more adverse than the transfer itself. However, neither an intention to make a transfer, nor a high likelihood of a transfer, is sufficient reason for concluding that the entity has no practical ability to avoid a transfer.

4.35   In some cases, it is uncertain whether an obligation exists. For example, if another party is seeking compensation for an entity's alleged act of wrongdoing, it might be uncertain whether the act occurred, whether the entity committed it or how the law applies. Until that existence uncertainty is resolved—for example, by a court ruling—it is uncertain whether the entity has an obligation to the party seeking compensation and, consequently, whether a liability exists. (Paragraph 5.14 discusses recognition of liabilities whose existence is uncertain.)

Transfer of an economic resource

4.36   The second criterion for a liability is that the obligation is to transfer an economic resource.

4.37   To satisfy this criterion, the obligation must have the potential to require the entity to transfer an economic resource to another party (or parties). For that potential to exist, it does not need to be certain, or even likely, that the entity will be required to transfer an economic resource—the transfer may, for example, be required only if a specified uncertain future event occurs. It is only necessary that the obligation already exists and that, in at least one circumstance, it would require the entity to transfer an economic resource.

4.38   An obligation can meet the definition of a liability even if the probability of a transfer of an economic resource is low. Nevertheless, that low probability might affect decisions about what information to provide about the liability and how to provide that information, including decisions about whether the liability is recognised (see paragraphs 5.15–5.17) and how it is measured.

4.39   Obligations to transfer an economic resource include, for example:

   (a)   obligations to pay cash.

   (b)   obligations to deliver goods or provide services.

   (c)   obligations to exchange economic resources with another party on unfavourable terms. Such obligations include, for example, a forward contract to sell an economic resource on terms that are currently unfavourable or an option that entitles another party to buy an economic resource from the entity.

   (d)   obligations to transfer an economic resource if a specified uncertain future event occurs.

   (e)   obligations to issue a financial instrument if that financial instrument will oblige the entity to transfer an economic resource.

4.40   Instead of fulfilling an obligation to transfer an economic resource to the party that has a right to receive that resource, entities sometimes decide to, for example:

   (a)   settle the obligation by negotiating a release from the obligation;

(b)   transfer the obligation to a third party; or

(c)   replace that obligation to transfer an economic resource with another obligation by entering into a new transaction.

4.41   In the situations described in paragraph 4.40, an entity has the obligation to transfer an economic resource until it has settled, transferred or replaced that obligation.

Present obligation as a result of past events

4.42   The third criterion for a liability is that the obligation is a present obligation that exists as a result of past events.

4.43   A present obligation exists as a result of past events only if:

(a)   the entity has already obtained economic benefits or taken an action; and

(b)   as a consequence, the entity will or may have to transfer an economic resource that it would not otherwise have had to transfer.

4.44   The economic benefits obtained could include, for example, goods or services. The action taken could include, for example, operating a particular business or operating in a particular market. If economic benefits are obtained, or an action is taken, over time, the resulting present obligation may accumulate over that time.

4.45   If new legislation is enacted, a present obligation arises only when, as a consequence of obtaining economic benefits or taking an action to which that legislation applies, an entity will or may have to transfer an economic resource that it would not otherwise have had to transfer. The enactment of legislation is not in itself sufficient to give an entity a present obligation. Similarly, an entity's customary practice, published policy or specific statement of the type mentioned in paragraph 4.31 gives rise to a present obligation only when, as a consequence of obtaining economic benefits, or taking an action, to which that practice, policy or statement applies, the entity will or may have to transfer an economic resource that it would not otherwise have had to transfer.

4.46   A present obligation can exist even if a transfer of economic resources cannot be enforced until some point in the future. For example, a contractual liability to pay cash may exist now even if the contract does not require a payment until a future date. Similarly, a contractual obligation for an entity to perform work at a future date may exist now even if the counterparty cannot require the entity to perform the work until that future date.

4.47   An entity does not yet have a present obligation to transfer an economic resource if it has not yet satisfied the criteria in paragraph 4.43, that is, if it has not yet obtained economic benefits, or taken an action, that would or could require the entity to transfer an economic resource that it would not otherwise have had to transfer. For example, if an entity has entered into a contract to pay an employee a salary in exchange for receiving the employee's services, the entity does not have a present obligation to pay the salary until it has received the employee's services. Before then the contract is executory—the entity has a combined right and obligation to exchange future salary for future employee services (see paragraphs 4.56–4.58).

Assets and liabilities

Unit of account

4.48 The unit of account is the right or the group of rights, the obligation or the group of obligations, or the group of rights and obligations, to which recognition criteria and measurement concepts are applied.

4.49 A unit of account is selected for an asset or liability when considering how recognition criteria and measurement concepts will apply to that asset or liability and to the related income and expenses. In some circumstances, it may be appropriate to select one unit of account for recognition and a different unit of account for measurement. For example, contracts may sometimes be recognised individually but measured as part of a portfolio of contracts. For presentation and disclosure, assets, liabilities, income and expenses may need to be aggregated or separated into components.

4.50 If an entity transfers part of an asset or part of a liability, the unit of account may change at that time, so that the transferred component and the retained component become separate units of account (see paragraphs 5.26–5.33).

4.51 A unit of account is selected to provide useful information, which implies that:

    (a) the information provided about the asset or liability and about any related income and expenses must be relevant. Treating a group of rights and obligations as a single unit of account may provide more relevant information than treating each right or obligation as a separate unit of account if, for example, those rights and obligations:

        (i) cannot be or are unlikely to be the subject of separate transactions;

        (ii) cannot or are unlikely to expire in different patterns;

        (iii) have similar economic characteristics and risks and hence are likely to have similar implications for the prospects for future net cash inflows to the entity or net cash outflows from the entity; or

        (iv) are used together in the business activities conducted by an entity to produce cash flows and are measured by reference to estimates of their interdependent future cash flows.

    (b) the information provided about the asset or liability and about any related income and expenses must faithfully represent the substance of the transaction or other event from which they have arisen. Therefore, it may be necessary to treat rights or obligations arising from different sources as a single unit of account, or to separate the rights or obligations arising from a single source (see paragraph 4.62). Equally, to provide a faithful representation of unrelated rights and obligations, it may be necessary to recognise and measure them separately.

4.52   Just as cost constrains other financial reporting decisions, it also constrains the selection of a unit of account. Hence, in selecting a unit of account, it is important to consider whether the benefits of the information provided to users of financial statements by selecting that unit of account are likely to justify the costs of providing and using that information. In general, the costs associated with recognising and measuring assets, liabilities, income and expenses increase as the size of the unit of account decreases. Hence, in general, rights or obligations arising from the same source are separated only if the resulting information is more useful and the benefits outweigh the costs.

4.53   Sometimes, both rights and obligations arise from the same source. For example, some contracts establish both rights and obligations for each of the parties. If those rights and obligations are interdependent and cannot be separated, they constitute a single inseparable asset or liability and hence form a single unit of account. For example, this is the case with executory contracts (see paragraph 4.57). Conversely, if rights are separable from obligations, it may sometimes be appropriate to group the rights separately from the obligations, resulting in the identification of one or more separate assets and liabilities. In other cases, it may be more appropriate to group separable rights and obligations in a single unit of account treating them as a single asset or a single liability.

4.54   Treating a set of rights and obligations as a single unit of account differs from offsetting assets and liabilities (see paragraph 7.10).

4.55   Possible units of account include:

(a)   an individual right or individual obligation;

(b)   all rights, all obligations, or all rights and all obligations, arising from a single source, for example, a contract;

(c)   a subgroup of those rights and/or obligations—for example, a subgroup of rights over an item of property, plant and equipment for which the useful life and pattern of consumption differ from those of the other rights over that item;

(d)   a group of rights and/or obligations arising from a portfolio of similar items;

(e)   a group of rights and/or obligations arising from a portfolio of dissimilar items—for example, a portfolio of assets and liabilities to be disposed of in a single transaction; and

(f)   a risk exposure within a portfolio of items—if a portfolio of items is subject to a common risk, some aspects of the accounting for that portfolio could focus on the aggregate exposure to that risk within the portfolio.

Executory contracts

4.56   An executory contract is a contract, or a portion of a contract, that is equally unperformed – neither party has fulfilled any of its obligations, or both parties have partially fulfilled their obligations to an equal extent.

4.57   An executory contract establishes a combined right and obligation to exchange economic resources. The right and obligation are interdependent and cannot be separated. Hence, the combined right and obligation constitute a single asset or liability. The entity has an asset if the terms of the exchange are currently favourable; it has a liability if the terms of the exchange are currently unfavourable. Whether such an asset or liability is included in the financial statements depends on both the recognition criteria (see Chapter 5) and the measurement basis (see Chapter 6) selected for the asset or liability, including, if applicable, any test for whether the contract is onerous.

4.58   To the extent that either party fulfils its obligations under the contract, the contract is no longer executory. If the reporting entity performs first under the contract, that performance is the event that changes the reporting entity's right and obligation to exchange economic resources into a right to receive an economic resource. That right is an asset. If the other party performs first, that performance is the event that changes the reporting entity's right and obligation to exchange economic resources into an obligation to transfer an economic resource. That obligation is a liability.

Substance of contractual rights and contractual obligations

4.59   The terms of a contract create rights and obligations for an entity that is a party to that contract. To represent those rights and obligations faithfully, financial statements report their substance (see paragraph 2.12). In some cases, the substance of the rights and obligations is clear from the legal form of the contract. In other cases, the terms of the contract or a group or series of contracts require analysis to identify the substance of the rights and obligations.

4.60   All terms in a contract – whether explicit or implicit – are considered unless they have no substance. Implicit terms could include, for example, obligations imposed by statute, such as statutory warranty obligations imposed on entities that enter into contracts to sell goods to customers.

4.61   Terms that have no substance are disregarded. A term has no substance if it has no discernible effect on the economics of the contract. Terms that have no substance could include, for example:

(a)   terms that bind neither party; or

(b)   rights, including options, that the holder will not have the practical ability to exercise in any circumstances.

4.62   A group or series of contracts may achieve or be designed to achieve an overall commercial effect. To report the substance of such contracts, it may be necessary to treat rights and obligations arising from that group or series of contracts as a single unit of account. For example, if the rights or obligations in one contract merely nullify all the rights or obligations in another contract entered into at the same time with the same counterparty, the combined effect is that the two contracts create no rights or obligations. Conversely, if a single contract creates two or more sets of rights or obligations that could have been created through two or more separate contracts, an entity may need to account for each set as if it arose from separate contracts in order to faithfully represent the rights and obligations (see paragraphs 4.48–4.55).

Definition of equity

4.63   Equity is the residual interest in the assets of the entity after deducting all its liabilities.

4.64   Equity claims are claims on the residual interest in the assets of the entity after deducting all its liabilities. In other words, they are claims against the entity that do not meet the definition of a liability. Such claims may be established by contract, legislation or similar means, and include, to the extent that they do not meet the definition of a liability:

(a)   shares of various types, issued by the entity; and

(b)   some obligations of the entity to issue another equity claim.

4.65   Different classes of equity claims, such as ordinary shares and preference shares, may confer on their holders different rights, for example, rights to receive some or all of the following from the entity:

(a)   dividends, if the entity decides to pay dividends to eligible holders;

(b)   the proceeds from satisfying the equity claims, either in full on liquidation, or in part at other times; or

(c)   other equity claims.

4.66   Sometimes, legal, regulatory or other requirements affect particular components of equity, such as share capital or retained earnings. For example, some such requirements permit an entity to make distributions to holders of equity claims only if the entity has sufficient reserves that those requirements specify as being distributable.

4.67   Business activities are often undertaken by entities such as sole proprietorships, partnerships, trusts or various types of government business undertakings. The legal and regulatory frameworks for such entities are often different from frameworks that apply to corporate entities. For example, there may be few, if any, restrictions on the distribution to holders of equity claims against such entities. Nevertheless, the definition of equity in paragraph 4.63 of the *Conceptual Framework* applies to all reporting entities.

Definitions of income and expenses

4.68   Income is increases in assets, or decreases in liabilities, that result in increases in equity, other than those relating to contributions from holders of equity claims.

4.69   Expenses are decreases in assets, or increases in liabilities, that result in decreases in equity, other than those relating to distributions to holders of equity claims.

4.70   It follows from these definitions of income and expenses that contributions from holders of equity claims are not income, and distributions to holders of equity claims are not expenses.

4.71   Income and expenses are the elements of financial statements that relate to an entity's financial performance. Users of financial statements need information about both an entity's financial position and its financial performance. Hence, although income and expenses are defined in terms of changes in assets and liabilities, information about income and expenses is just as important as information about assets and liabilities.

4.72   Different transactions and other events generate income and expenses with different characteristics. Providing information separately about income and expenses with different characteristics can help users of financial statements to understand the entity's financial performance (see paragraphs 7.14–7.19).

Contents

The recognition process

5.1　　Recognition is the process of capturing for inclusion in the statement of financial position or the statement(s) of financial performance an item that meets the definition of one of the elements of financial statements – an asset, a liability, equity, income or expenses. Recognition involves depicting the item in one of those statements – either alone or in aggregation with other items – in words and by a monetary amount, and including that amount in one or more totals in that statement. The amount at which an asset, a liability or equity is recognised in the statement of financial position is referred to as its 'carrying amount'.

5.2　　The statement of financial position and statement(s) of financial performance depict an entity's recognised assets, liabilities, equity, income and expenses in structured summaries that are designed to make financial information comparable and understandable. An important feature of the structures of those summaries is that the amounts recognised in a statement are included in the totals and, if applicable, subtotals that link the items recognised in the statement.

5.3　　Recognition links the elements, the statement of financial position and the statement(s) of financial performance as follows (see Diagram 5.1):

　　(a)　　in the statement of financial position at the beginning and end of the reporting period, total assets minus total liabilities equal total equity; and

　　(b)　　recognised changes in equity during the reporting period comprise:

　　　　(i)　　income minus expenses recognised in the statement(s) of financial performance; plus

　　　　(ii)　　contributions from holders of equity claims, minus distributions to holders of equity claims.

5.4　　The statements are linked because the recognition of one item (or a change in its carrying amount) requires the recognition or derecognition of one or more other items (or changes in the carrying amount of one or more other items). For example:

　　(a)　　the recognition of income occurs at the same time as:

　　　　(i)　　the initial recognition of an asset, or an increase in the carrying amount of an asset; or

　　　　(ii)　　the derecognition of a liability, or a decrease in the carrying amount of a liability.

　　(b)　　the recognition of expenses occurs at the same time as:

　　　　(i)　　the initial recognition of a liability, or an increase in the carrying amount of a liability; or

　　　　(ii)　　the derecognition of an asset, or a decrease in the carrying amount of an asset.

Diagram 5.1: How recognition links the elements of financial statements

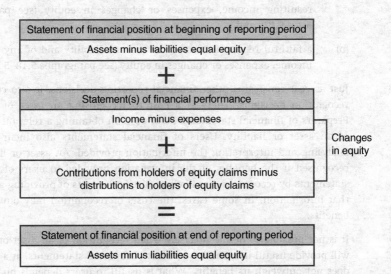

5.5   The initial recognition of assets or liabilities arising from transactions or other events may result in the simultaneous recognition of both income and related expenses. For example, the sale of goods for cash results in the recognition of both income (from the recognition of one asset—the cash) and an expense (from the derecognition of another asset—the goods sold). The simultaneous recognition of income and related expenses is sometimes referred to as the matching of costs with income. Application of the concepts in the *Conceptual Framework* leads to such matching when it arises from the recognition of changes in assets and liabilities. However, matching of costs with income is not an objective of the *Conceptual Framework*. The *Conceptual Framework* does not allow the recognition in the statement of financial position of items that do not meet the definition of an asset, a liability or equity.

Recognition criteria

5.6   Only items that meet the definition of an asset, a liability or equity are recognised in the statement of financial position. Similarly, only items that meet the definition of income or expenses are recognised in the statement(s) of financial performance. However, not all items that meet the definition of one of those elements are recognised.

5.7   Not recognising an item that meets the definition of one of the elements makes the statement of financial position and the statement(s) of financial performance less complete and can exclude useful information from financial statements. On the other hand, in some circumstances, recognising some items that meet the definition of one of the elements would not provide useful information. An asset or liability is recognised only if recognition of that asset or liability and of any resulting income, expenses or changes in equity provides users of financial statements with information that is useful, ie with:

(a)   relevant information about the asset or liability and about any resulting income, expenses or changes in equity (see paragraphs 5.12–5.17); and

(b)   a faithful representation of the asset or liability and of any resulting income, expenses or changes in equity (see paragraphs 5.18–5.25).

5.8   Just as cost constrains other financial reporting decisions, it also constrains recognition decisions. There is a cost to recognising an asset or liability. Preparers of financial statements incur costs in obtaining a relevant measure of an asset or liability. Users of financial statements also incur costs in analysing and interpreting the information provided. An asset or liability is recognised if the benefits of the information provided to users of financial statements by recognition are likely to justify the costs of providing and using that information. In some cases, the costs of recognition may outweigh its benefits.

5.9   It is not possible to define precisely when recognition of an asset or liability will provide useful information to users of financial statements, at a cost that does not outweigh its benefits. What is useful to users depends on the item and the facts and circumstances. Consequently, judgement is required when deciding whether to recognise an item, and thus recognition requirements may need to vary between and within Standards.

5.10   It is important when making decisions about recognition to consider the information that would be given if an asset or liability were not recognised. For example, if no asset is recognised when expenditure is incurred, an expense is recognised. Over time, recognising the expense may, in some cases, provide useful information, for example, information that enables users of financial statements to identify trends.

5.11   Even if an item meeting the definition of an asset or liability is not recognised, an entity may need to provide information about that item in the notes. It is important to consider how to make such information sufficiently visible to compensate for the item's absence from the structured summary provided by the statement of financial position and, if applicable, the statement(s) of financial performance.

Relevance

5.12   Information about assets, liabilities, equity, income and expenses is relevant to users of financial statements. However, recognition of a particular asset or liability and any resulting income, expenses or changes in equity may not always provide relevant information. That may be the case if, for example:

(a)   it is uncertain whether an asset or liability exists (see paragraph 5.14); or

(b)   an asset or liability exists, but the probability of an inflow or outflow of economic benefits is low (see paragraphs 5.15–5.17).

5.13   The presence of one or both of the factors described in paragraph 5.12 does not lead automatically to a conclusion that the information provided by recognition lacks relevance. Moreover, factors other than those described in paragraph 5.12 may also affect the conclusion. It may be a combination of factors and not any single factor that determines whether recognition provides relevant information.

Existence uncertainty

5.14   Paragraphs 4.13 and 4.35 discuss cases in which it is uncertain whether an asset or liability exists. In some cases, that uncertainty, possibly combined with a low probability of inflows or outflows of economic benefits and an exceptionally wide range of possible outcomes, may mean that the recognition of an asset or liability, necessarily measured at a single amount, would not provide relevant information. Whether or not the asset or liability is recognised, explanatory information about the uncertainties associated with it may need to be provided in the financial statements.

Low probability of an inflow or outflow of economic benefits

5.15   An asset or liability can exist even if the probability of an inflow or outflow of economic benefits is low (see paragraphs 4.15 and 4.38).

5.16   If the probability of an inflow or outflow of economic benefits is low, the most relevant information about the asset or liability may be information about the magnitude of the possible inflows or outflows, their possible timing and the factors affecting the probability of their occurrence. The typical location for such information is in the notes.

5.17   Even if the probability of an inflow or outflow of economic benefits is low, recognition of the asset or liability may provide relevant information beyond the information described in paragraph 5.16. Whether that is the case may depend on a variety of factors. For example:

   (a)   if an asset is acquired or a liability is incurred in an exchange transaction on market terms, its cost generally reflects the probability of an inflow or outflow of economic benefits. Thus, that cost may be relevant information, and is generally readily available. Furthermore, not recognising the asset or liability would result in the recognition of expenses or income at the time of the exchange, which might not be a faithful representation of the transaction (see paragraph 5.25(a)).

   (b)   if an asset or liability arises from an event that is not an exchange transaction, recognition of the asset or liability typically results in recognition of income or expenses. If there is only a low probability that the asset or liability will result in an inflow or outflow of economic benefits, users of financial statements might not regard the recognition of the asset and income, or the liability and expenses, as providing relevant information.

Faithful representation

5.18   Recognition of a particular asset or liability is appropriate if it provides not only relevant information, but also a faithful representation of that asset or liability and of any resulting income, expenses or changes in equity. Whether a faithful representation can be provided may be affected by the level of measurement uncertainty associated with the asset or liability or by other factors.

Measurement uncertainty

5.19   For an asset or liability to be recognised, it must be measured. In many cases, such measures must be estimated and are therefore subject to measurement uncertainty. As noted in paragraph 2.19, the use of reasonable estimates is an essential part of the preparation of financial information and does not undermine the usefulness of the information if the estimates are clearly and accurately described and explained. Even a high level of measurement uncertainty does not necessarily prevent such an estimate from providing useful information.

5.20   In some cases, the level of uncertainty involved in estimating a measure of an asset or liability may be so high that it may be questionable whether the estimate would provide a sufficiently faithful representation of that asset or liability and of any resulting income, expenses or changes in equity. The level of measurement uncertainty may be so high if, for example, the only way of estimating that measure of the asset or liability is by using cash-flow-based measurement techniques and, in addition, one or more of the following circumstances exists:

(a)   the range of possible outcomes is exceptionally wide and the probability of each outcome is exceptionally difficult to estimate.

(b)   the measure is exceptionally sensitive to small changes in estimates of the probability of different outcomes—for example, if the probability of future cash inflows or outflows occurring is exceptionally low, but the magnitude of those cash inflows or outflows will be exceptionally high if they occur.

(c)   measuring the asset or liability requires exceptionally difficult or exceptionally subjective allocations of cash flows that do not relate solely to the asset or liability being measured.

5.21   In some of the cases described in paragraph 5.20, the most useful information may be the measure that relies on the highly uncertain estimate, accompanied by a description of the estimate and an explanation of the uncertainties that affect it. This is especially likely to be the case if that measure is the most relevant measure of the asset or liability. In other cases, if that information would not provide a sufficiently faithful representation of the asset or liability and of any resulting income, expenses or changes in equity, the most useful information may be a different measure (accompanied by any necessary descriptions and explanations) that is slightly less relevant but is subject to lower measurement uncertainty.

5.22   In limited circumstances, all relevant measures of an asset or liability that are available (or can be obtained) may be subject to such high measurement uncertainty that none would provide useful information about the asset or liability (and any resulting income, expenses or changes in equity), even if the measure were accompanied by a description of the estimates made in producing it and an explanation of the uncertainties that affect those estimates. In those limited circumstances, the asset or liability would not be recognised.

5.23   Whether or not an asset or liability is recognised, a faithful representation of the asset or liability may need to include explanatory information about the uncertainties associated with the asset or liability's existence or measurement, or with its outcome—the amount or timing of any inflow or outflow of economic benefits that will ultimately result from it (see paragraphs 6.60–6.62).

Other factors

5.24   Faithful representation of a recognised asset, liability, equity, income or expenses involves not only recognition of that item, but also its measurement as well as presentation and disclosure of information about it (see Chapters 6–7).

5.25   Hence, when assessing whether the recognition of an asset or liability can provide a faithful representation of the asset or liability, it is necessary to consider not merely its description and measurement in the statement of financial position, but also:

(a)   the depiction of resulting income, expenses and changes in equity. For example, if an entity acquires an asset in exchange for consideration, not recognising the asset would result in recognising expenses and would reduce the entity's profit and equity. In some cases, for example, if the entity does not consume the asset immediately, that result could provide a misleading representation that the entity's financial position has deteriorated.

(b)   whether related assets and liabilities are recognised. If they are not recognised, recognition may create a recognition inconsistency (accounting mismatch). That may not provide an understandable or faithful representation of the overall effect of the transaction or other event giving rise to the asset or liability, even if explanatory information is provided in the notes.

(c)   presentation and disclosure of information about the asset or liability, and resulting income, expenses or changes in equity. A complete depiction includes all information necessary for a user of financial statements to understand the economic phenomenon depicted, including all necessary descriptions and explanations. Hence, presentation and disclosure of related information can enable a recognised amount to form part of a faithful representation of an asset, a liability, equity, income or expenses.

Derecognition

5.26 Derecognition is the removal of all or part of a recognised asset or liability from an entity's statement of financial position. Derecognition normally occurs when that item no longer meets the definition of an asset or of a liability:

(a) for an asset, derecognition normally occurs when the entity loses control of all or part of the recognised asset; and

(b) for a liability, derecognition normally occurs when the entity no longer has a present obligation for all or part of the recognised liability.

5.27 Accounting requirements for derecognition aim to faithfully represent both:

(a) any assets and liabilities retained after the transaction or other event that led to the derecognition (including any asset or liability acquired, incurred or created as part of the transaction or other event); and

(b) the change in the entity's assets and liabilities as a result of that transaction or other event.

5.28 The aims described in paragraph 5.27 are normally achieved by:

(a) derecognising any assets or liabilities that have expired or have been consumed, collected, fulfilled or transferred, and recognising any resulting income and expenses. In the rest of this chapter, the term 'transferred component' refers to all those assets and liabilities;

(b) continuing to recognise the assets or liabilities retained, referred to as the 'retained component', if any. That retained component becomes a unit of account separate from the transferred component. Accordingly, no income or expenses are recognised on the retained component as a result of the derecognition of the transferred component, unless the derecognition results in a change in the measurement requirements applicable to the retained component; and

(c) applying one or more of the following procedures, if that is necessary to achieve one or both of the aims described in paragraph 5.27:

(i) presenting any retained component separately in the statement of financial position;

(ii) presenting separately in the statement(s) of financial performance any income and expenses recognised as a result of the derecognition of the transferred component; or

(iii) providing explanatory information.

5.29 In some cases, an entity might appear to transfer an asset or liability, but that asset or liability might nevertheless remain an asset or liability of the entity. For example:

(a)   if an entity has apparently transferred an asset but retains exposure to significant positive or negative variations in the amount of economic benefits that may be produced by the asset, this sometimes indicates that the entity might continue to control that asset (see paragraph 4.24); or

(b)   if an entity has transferred an asset to another party that holds the asset as an agent for the entity, the transferor still controls the asset (see paragraph 4.25).

5.30   In the cases described in paragraph 5.29, derecognition of that asset or liability is not appropriate because it would not achieve either of the two aims described in paragraph 5.27.

5.31   When an entity no longer has a transferred component, derecognition of the transferred component faithfully represents that fact. However, in some of those cases, derecognition may not faithfully represent how much a transaction or other event changed the entity's assets or liabilities, even when supported by one or more of the procedures described in paragraph 5.28(c). In those cases, derecognition of the transferred component might imply that the entity's financial position has changed more significantly than it has. This might occur, for example:

(a)   if an entity has transferred an asset and, at the same time, entered into another transaction that results in a present right or present obligation to reacquire the asset. Such present rights or present obligations may arise from, for example, a forward contract, a written put option, or a purchased call option.

(b)   if an entity has retained exposure to significant positive or negative variations in the amount of economic benefits that may be produced by a transferred component that the entity no longer controls.

5.32   If derecognition is not sufficient to achieve both aims described in paragraph 5.27, even when supported by one or more of the procedures described in paragraph 5.28(c), those two aims might sometimes be achieved by continuing to recognise the transferred component. This has the following consequences:

(a)   no income or expenses are recognised on either the retained component or the transferred component as a result of the transaction or other event;

(b)   the proceeds received (or paid) upon transfer of the asset (or liability) are treated as a loan received (or given); and

(c)   separate presentation of the transferred component in the statement of financial position, or provision of explanatory information, is needed to depict the fact that the entity no longer has any rights or obligations arising from the transferred component. Similarly, it may be necessary to provide information about income or expenses arising from the transferred component after the transfer.

5.33   One case in which questions about derecognition arise is when a contract is modified in a way that reduces or eliminates existing rights or obligations. In deciding how to account for contract modifications, it is necessary to consider which unit of account provides users of financial statements with the most useful information about the assets and liabilities retained after the modification, and about how the modification changed the entity's assets and liabilities:

   (a)   if a contract modification only eliminates existing rights or obligations, the discussion in paragraphs 5.26–5.32 is considered in deciding whether to derecognise those rights or obligations;

   (b)   if a contract modification only adds new rights or obligations, it is necessary to decide whether to treat the added rights or obligations as a separate asset or liability, or as part of the same unit of account as the existing rights and obligations (see paragraphs 4.48–4.55); and

   (c)   if a contract modification both eliminates existing rights or obligations and adds new rights or obligations, it is necessary to consider both the separate and the combined effect of those modifications. In some such cases, the contract has been modified to such an extent that, in substance, the modification replaces the old asset or liability with a new asset or liability. In cases of such extensive modification, the entity may need to derecognise the original asset or liability, and recognise the new asset or liability.

Contents

Introduction

6.1 Elements recognised in financial statements are quantified in monetary terms. This requires the selection of a measurement basis. A measurement basis is an identified feature—for example, historical cost, fair value or fulfilment value—of an item being measured. Applying a measurement basis to an asset or liability creates a measure for that asset or liability and for related income and expenses.

6.2 Consideration of the qualitative characteristics of useful financial information and of the cost constraint is likely to result in the selection of different measurement bases for different assets, liabilities, income and expenses.

6.3 A Standard may need to describe how to implement the measurement basis selected in that Standard. That description could include:

(a) specifying techniques that may or must be used to estimate a measure applying a particular measurement basis;

(b) specifying a simplified measurement approach that is likely to provide information similar to that provided by a preferred measurement basis; or

(c) explaining how to modify a measurement basis, for example, by excluding from the fulfilment value of a liability the effect of the possibility that the entity may fail to fulfil that liability (own credit risk).

Measurement bases

Historical cost

6.4 Historical cost measures provide monetary information about assets, liabilities and related income and expenses, using information derived, at least in part, from the price of the transaction or other event that gave rise to them. Unlike current value, historical cost does not reflect changes in values, except to the extent that those changes relate to impairment of an asset or a liability becoming onerous (see paragraphs 6.7(c) and 6.8(b)).

6.5 The historical cost of an asset when it is acquired or created is the value of the costs incurred in acquiring or creating the asset, comprising the consideration paid to acquire or create the asset plus transaction costs. The historical cost of a liability when it is incurred or taken on is the value of the consideration received to incur or take on the liability minus transaction costs.

6.6 When an asset is acquired or created, or a liability is incurred or taken on, as a result of an event that is not a transaction on market terms (see paragraph 6.80), it may not be possible to identify a cost, or the cost may not provide relevant information about the asset or liability. In some such cases, a current value of the asset or liability is used as a deemed cost on initial recognition and that deemed cost is then used as a starting point for subsequent measurement at historical cost.

6.7   The historical cost of an asset is updated over time to depict, if applicable:

(a)   the consumption of part or all of the economic resource that constitutes the asset (depreciation or amortisation);

(b)   payments received that extinguish part or all of the asset;

(c)   the effect of events that cause part or all of the historical cost of the asset to be no longer recoverable (impairment); and

(d)   accrual of interest to reflect any financing component of the asset.

6.8   The historical cost of a liability is updated over time to depict, if applicable:

(a)   fulfilment of part or all of the liability, for example, by making payments that extinguish part or all of the liability or by satisfying an obligation to deliver goods;

(b)   the effect of events that increase the value of the obligation to transfer the economic resources needed to fulfil the liability to such an extent that the liability becomes onerous. A liability is onerous if the historical cost is no longer sufficient to depict the obligation to fulfil the liability; and

(c)   accrual of interest to reflect any financing component of the liability.

6.9   One way to apply a historical cost measurement basis to financial assets and financial liabilities is to measure them at amortised cost. The amortised cost of a financial asset or financial liability reflects estimates of future cash flows, discounted at a rate determined at initial recognition. For variable rate instruments, the discount rate is updated to reflect changes in the variable rate. The amortised cost of a financial asset or financial liability is updated over time to depict subsequent changes, such as the accrual of interest, the impairment of a financial asset and receipts or payments.

Current value

6.10   Current value measures provide monetary information about assets, liabilities and related income and expenses, using information updated to reflect conditions at the measurement date. Because of the updating, current values of assets and liabilities reflect changes, since the previous measurement date, in estimates of cash flows and other factors reflected in those current values (see paragraphs 6.14–6.15 and 6.20). Unlike historical cost, the current value of an asset or liability is not derived, even in part, from the price of the transaction or other event that gave rise to the asset or liability.

6.11   Current value measurement bases include:

(a)   fair value (see paragraphs 6.12–6.16);

(b)   value in use for assets and fulfilment value for liabilities (see paragraphs 6.17–6.20); and

(c)   current cost (see paragraphs 6.21–6.22).

Fair value

6.12 Fair value is the price that would be received to sell an asset, or paid to transfer a liability, in an orderly transaction between market participants at the measurement date.

6.13 Fair value reflects the perspective of market participants—participants in a market to which the entity has access. The asset or liability is measured using the same assumptions that market participants would use when pricing the asset or liability if those market participants act in their economic best interest.

6.14 In some cases, fair value can be determined directly by observing prices in an active market. In other cases, it is determined indirectly using measurement techniques, for example, cash-flow-based measurement techniques (see paragraphs 6.91–6.95), reflecting all the following factors:

(a) estimates of future cash flows.

(b) possible variations in the estimated amount or timing of future cash flows for the asset or liability being measured, caused by the uncertainty inherent in the cash flows.

(c) the time value of money.

(d) the price for bearing the uncertainty inherent in the cash flows (a risk premium or risk discount). The price for bearing that uncertainty depends on the extent of that uncertainty. It also reflects the fact that investors would generally pay less for an asset (and generally require more for taking on a liability) that has uncertain cash flows than for an asset (or liability) whose cash flows are certain.

(e) other factors, for example, liquidity, if market participants would take those factors into account in the circumstances.

6.15 The factors mentioned in paragraphs 6.14(b) and 6.14(d) include the possibility that a counterparty may fail to fulfil its liability to the entity (credit risk), or that the entity may fail to fulfil its liability (own credit risk).

6.16 Because fair value is not derived, even in part, from the price of the transaction or other event that gave rise to the asset or liability, fair value is not increased by the transaction costs incurred when acquiring the asset and is not decreased by the transaction costs incurred when the liability is incurred or taken on. In addition, fair value does not reflect the transaction costs that would be incurred on the ultimate disposal of the asset or on transferring or settling the liability.

Value in use and fulfilment value

6.17 Value in use is the present value of the cash flows, or other economic benefits, that an entity expects to derive from the use of an asset and from its ultimate disposal. Fulfilment value is the present value of the cash, or other economic resources, that an entity expects to be obliged to transfer as it fulfils a liability. Those amounts of cash or other economic resources include not only the amounts to be transferred to the liability counterparty, but also the amounts that the entity expects to be obliged to transfer to other parties to enable it to fulfil the liability.

6.18 Because value in use and fulfilment value are based on future cash flows, they do not include transaction costs incurred on acquiring an asset or taking on a liability. However, value in use and fulfilment value include the present value of any transaction costs an entity expects to incur on the ultimate disposal of the asset or on fulfilling the liability.

6.19 Value in use and fulfilment value reflect entity-specific assumptions rather than assumptions by market participants. In practice, there may sometimes be little difference between the assumptions that market participants would use and those that an entity itself uses.

6.20 Value in use and fulfilment value cannot be observed directly and are determined using cash-flow-based measurement techniques (see paragraphs 6.91–6.95). Value in use and fulfilment value reflect the same factors described for fair value in paragraph 6.14, but from an entity-specific perspective rather than from a market-participant perspective.

Current cost

6.21 The current cost of an asset is the cost of an equivalent asset at the measurement date, comprising the consideration that would be paid at the measurement date plus the transaction costs that would be incurred at that date. The current cost of a liability is the consideration that would be received for an equivalent liability at the measurement date minus the transaction costs that would be incurred at that date. Current cost, like historical cost, is an entry value: it reflects prices in the market in which the entity would acquire the asset or would incur the liability. Hence, it is different from fair value, value in use and fulfilment value, which are exit values. However, unlike historical cost, current cost reflects conditions at the measurement date.

6.22 In some cases, current cost cannot be determined directly by observing prices in an active market and must be determined indirectly by other means. For example, if prices are available only for new assets, the current cost of a used asset might need to be estimated by adjusting the current price of a new asset to reflect the current age and condition of the asset held by the entity.

Information provided by particular measurement bases

6.23 When selecting a measurement basis, it is important to consider the nature of the information that the measurement basis will produce in both the statement of financial position and the statement(s) of financial performance. Table 6.1 summarises that information and paragraphs 6.24–6.42 provide additional discussion.

Historical cost

6.24   Information provided by measuring an asset or liability at historical cost may be relevant to users of financial statements, because historical cost uses information derived, at least in part, from the price of the transaction or other event that gave rise to the asset or liability.

6.25   Normally, if an entity acquired an asset in a recent transaction on market terms, the entity expects that the asset will provide sufficient economic benefits that the entity will at least recover the cost of the asset. Similarly, if a liability was incurred or taken on as a result of a recent transaction on market terms, the entity expects that the value of the obligation to transfer economic resources to fulfil the liability will normally be no more than the value of the consideration received minus transaction costs. Hence, measuring an asset or liability at historical cost in such cases provides relevant information about both the asset or liability and the price of the transaction that gave rise to that asset or liability.

6.26   Because historical cost is reduced to reflect consumption of an asset and its impairment, the amount expected to be recovered from an asset measured at historical cost is at least as great as its carrying amount. Similarly, because the historical cost of a liability is increased when it becomes onerous, the value of the obligation to transfer the economic resources needed to fulfil the liability is no more than the carrying amount of the liability.

6.27   If an asset other than a financial asset is measured at historical cost, consumption or sale of the asset, or of part of the asset, gives rise to an expense measured at the historical cost of the asset, or of part of the asset, consumed or sold.

6.28   The expense arising from the sale of an asset is recognised at the same time as the consideration for that sale is recognised as income. The difference between the income and the expense is the margin resulting from the sale. Expenses arising from consumption of an asset can be compared to related income to provide information about margins.

6.29   Similarly, if a liability other than a financial liability was incurred or taken on in exchange for consideration and is measured at historical cost, the fulfilment of all or part of the liability gives rise to income measured at the value of the consideration received for the part fulfilled. The difference between that income and the expenses incurred in fulfilling the liability is the margin resulting from the fulfilment.

6.30   Information about the cost of assets sold or consumed, including goods and services consumed immediately (see paragraph 4.8), and about the consideration received, may have predictive value. That information can be used as an input in predicting future margins from the future sale of goods (including goods not currently held by the entity) and services and hence to assess the entity's prospects for future net cash inflows. To assess an entity's prospects for future cash flows, users of financial statements often focus on the entity's prospects for generating future margins over many periods, not just on its prospects for generating margins from goods already held. Income and expenses measured at historical cost may also have confirmatory value because they may provide feedback to users of financial statements about their previous predictions of cash flows or of margins. Information about the cost of assets sold or consumed may also help in an assessment of how efficiently and effectively the entity's management has discharged its responsibilities to use the entity's economic resources.

6.31   For similar reasons, information about interest earned on assets, and interest incurred on liabilities, measured at amortised cost may have predictive and confirmatory value.

Current value

Fair value

6.32   Information provided by measuring assets and liabilities at fair value may have predictive value because fair value reflects market participants' current expectations about the amount, timing and uncertainty of future cash flows. These expectations are priced in a manner that reflects the current risk preferences of market participants. That information may also have confirmatory value by providing feedback about previous expectations.

6.33   Income and expenses reflecting market participants' current expectations may have some predictive value, because such income and expenses can be used as an input in predicting future income and expenses. Such income and expenses may also help in an assessment of how efficiently and effectively the entity's management has discharged its responsibilities to use the entity's economic resources.

6.34   A change in the fair value of an asset or liability can result from various factors identified in paragraph 6.14. When those factors have different characteristics, identifying separately income and expenses that result from those factors can provide useful information to users of financial statements (see paragraph 7.14(b)).

6.35   If an entity acquired an asset in one market and determines fair value using prices in a different market (the market in which the entity would sell the asset), any difference between the prices in those two markets is recognised as income when that fair value is first determined.

6.36   Sale of an asset or transfer of a liability would normally be for consideration of an amount similar to its fair value, if the transaction were to occur in the market that was the source for the prices used when measuring that fair value. In those cases, if the asset or liability is measured at fair value, the net income or net expenses arising at the time of the sale or transfer would usually be small, unless the effect of transaction costs is significant.

Value in use and fulfilment value

6.37   Value in use provides information about the present value of the estimated cash flows from the use of an asset and from its ultimate disposal. This information may have predictive value because it can be used in assessing the prospects for future net cash inflows.

6.38   Fulfilment value provides information about the present value of the estimated cash flows needed to fulfil a liability. Hence, fulfilment value may have predictive value, particularly if the liability will be fulfilled, rather than transferred or settled by negotiation.

6.39   Updated estimates of value in use or fulfilment value, combined with information about estimates of the amount, timing and uncertainty of future cash flows, may also have confirmatory value because they provide feedback about previous estimates of value in use or fulfilment value.

Current cost

6.40   Information about assets and liabilities measured at current cost may be relevant because current cost reflects the cost at which an equivalent asset could be acquired or created at the measurement date or the consideration that would be received for incurring or taking on an equivalent liability.

6.41   Like historical cost, current cost provides information about the cost of an asset consumed or about income from the fulfilment of liabilities. That information can be used to derive current margins and can be used as an input in predicting future margins. Unlike historical cost, current cost reflects prices prevailing at the time of consumption or fulfilment. When price changes are significant, margins based on current cost may be more useful for predicting future margins than margins based on historical cost.

6.42   To report the current cost of consumption (or current income from fulfilment), it is necessary to split the change in the carrying amount in the reporting period into the current cost of consumption (or current income from fulfilment), and the effect of changes in prices. The effect of a change in prices is sometimes referred to as a 'holding gain' or a 'holding loss'.

Table 6.1 – Summary of information provided by particular measurement bases

Assets

Statement of financial position				
	Historical cost	**Fair value (market-participant assumptions)**[a]	**Value in use (entity-specific assumptions)**[a]	**Current cost**
Carrying amount	Historical cost (including transaction costs), to the extent unconsumed or uncollected, and recoverable. (Includes interest accrued on any financing component.)	Price that would be received to sell the asset (without deducting transaction costs on disposal).	Present value of future cash flows from the use of the asset and from its ultimate disposal (after deducting present value of transaction costs on disposal).	Current cost (including transaction costs), to the extent unconsumed or uncollected, and recoverable.

Statement(s) of financial performance				
Event	**Historical cost**	**Fair value (market-participant assumptions)**	**Value in use (entity-specific assumptions)**	**Current cost**
Initial recognition[b]	—	Difference between consideration paid and fair value of the asset acquired.[c] Transaction costs on acquiring the asset.	Difference between consideration paid and value in use of the asset acquired. Transaction costs on acquiring the asset.	—
Sale or consumption of the asset[d], [e]	Expenses equal to historical cost of the asset sold or consumed. Income received. (Could be presented gross or net.) Expenses for transaction costs on selling the asset.	Expenses equal to fair value of the asset sold or consumed. Income received. (Could be presented gross or net.) Expenses for transaction costs on selling the asset.	Expenses equal to value in use of the asset sold or consumed. Income received. (Could be presented gross or net.)	Expenses equal to current cost of the asset sold or consumed. Income received. (Could be presented gross or net.) Expenses for transaction costs on selling the asset.

continued...

...continued

Statement(s) of financial performance				
Event	**Historical cost**	**Fair value (market-participant assumptions)**	**Value in use (entity-specific assumptions)**	**Current cost**
Interest income	Interest income, at historical rates, updated if the asset bears variable interest.	Reflected in income and expenses from changes in fair value. (Could be identified separately.)	Reflected in income and expenses from changes in value in use. (Could be identified separately.)	Interest income, at current rates.
Impairment	Expenses arising because historical cost is no longer recoverable.	Reflected in income and expenses from changes in fair value. (Could be identified separately.)	Reflected in income and expenses from changes in value in use. (Could be identified separately.)	Expenses arising because current cost is no longer recoverable.
Value changes	Not recognised, except to reflect an impairment. For financial assets—income and expenses from changes in estimated cash flows.	Reflected in income and expenses from changes in fair value.	Reflected in income and expenses from changes in value in use.	Income and expenses reflecting the effect of changes in prices (holding gains and holding losses).

(a) This column summarises the information provided if value in use is used as a measurement basis. However, as noted in paragraph 6.75, value in use may not be a practical measurement basis for regular remeasurements.

(b) Income or expenses may arise on the initial recognition of an asset not acquired on market terms.

(c) Income or expenses may arise if the market in which an asset is acquired is different from the market that is the source of the prices used when measuring the fair value of the asset.

(d) Consumption of the asset is typically reported through cost of sales, depreciation or amortisation.

(e) Income received is often equal to the consideration received but will depend on the measurement basis used for any related liability.

Liabilities

Statement of financial position			
	Historical cost	**Fair value (market-participant assumptions)**	**Fulfilment value (entity-specific assumptions)**	**Current cost**
Carrying amount	Consideration received (net of transaction costs) for taking on the unfulfilled part of the liability, increased by excess of estimated cash outflows over consideration received. (Includes interest accrued on any financing component.)	Price that would be paid to transfer the unfulfilled part of the liability (not including transaction costs that would be incurred on transfer).	Present value of future cash flows that will arise in fulfilling the unfulfilled part of the liability (including present value of transaction costs to be incurred in fulfilment or transfer).	Consideration (net of transaction costs) that would be currently received for taking on the unfulfilled part of the liability, increased by excess of estimated cash outflows over that consideration.

Statement(s) of financial performance			
Event	**Historical cost**	**Fair value (market-participant assumptions)**	**Fulfilment value (entity-specific assumptions)**	**Current cost**
Initial recognition[a]	—	Difference between consideration received and the fair value of the liability. [b] Transaction costs on incurring or taking on the liability.	Difference between consideration received and the fulfilment value of the liability. Transaction costs on incurring or taking on the liability.	—

continued...

...continued

Statement(s) of financial performance				
Event	Historical cost	Fair value (market-participant assumptions)	Fulfilment value (entity-specific assumptions)	Current cost
Fulfilment of the liability	Income equal to historical cost of the liability fulfilled (reflects historical consideration). Expenses for costs incurred in fulfilling the liability. (Could be presented net or gross.)	Income equal to fair value of the liability fulfilled. Expenses for costs incurred in fulfilling the liability. (Could be presented net or gross. If gross, historical consideration could be presented separately.)	Income equal to fulfilment value of the liability fulfilled. Expenses for costs incurred in fulfilling the liability. (Could be presented net or gross. If gross, historical consideration could be presented separately.)	Income equal to current cost of the liability fulfilled (reflects current consideration). Expenses for costs incurred in fulfilling the liability. (Could be presented net or gross. If gross, historical consideration could be presented separately.)
Transfer of the liability	Income equal to historical cost of the liability transferred (reflects historical consideration). Expenses for costs paid (including transaction costs) to transfer the liability. (Could be presented net or gross.)	Income equal to fair value of the liability transferred. Expenses for costs paid (including transaction costs) to transfer the liability. (Could be presented net or gross.)	Income equal to fulfilment value of the liability transferred. Expenses for costs paid (including transaction costs) to transfer the liability. (Could be presented net or gross.)	Income equal to current cost of the liability transferred (reflects current consideration). Expenses for costs paid (including transaction costs) to transfer the liability. (Could be presented net or gross.)
Interest expenses	Interest expenses, at historical rates, updated if the liability bears variable interest.	Reflected in income and expenses from changes in fair value. (Could be identified separately.)	Reflected in income and expenses from changes in fulfilment value. (Could be identified separately.)	Interest expenses, at current rates.

continued...

...continued

	Statement(s) of financial performance			
Event	Historical cost	Fair value (market-participant assumptions)	Fulfilment value (entity-specific assumptions)	Current cost
Effect of events that cause a liability to become onerous	Expenses equal to the excess of the estimated cash outflows over the historical cost of the liability, or a subsequent change in that excess.	Reflected in income and expenses from changes in fair value. (Could be identified separately.)	Reflected in income and expenses from changes in fulfilment value. (Could be identified separately.)	Expenses equal to the excess of the estimated cash outflows over the current cost of the liability, or a subsequent change in that excess.
Value changes	Not recognised except to the extent that the liability is onerous. For financial liabilities—income and expenses from changes in estimated cash flows.	Reflected in income and expenses from changes in fair value.	Reflected in income and expenses from changes in fulfilment value.	Income and expenses reflecting the effect of changes in prices (holding gains and holding losses).

(a) Income or expenses may arise on the initial recognition of a liability incurred or taken on not on market terms.

(b) Income or expenses may arise if the market in which a liability is incurred or taken on is different from the market that is the source of the prices used when measuring the fair value of the liability.

Factors to consider when selecting a measurement basis

6.43   In selecting a measurement basis for an asset or liability and for the related income and expenses, it is necessary to consider the nature of the information that the measurement basis will produce in both the statement of financial position and the statement(s) of financial performance (see paragraphs 6.23–6.42 and Table 6.1), as well as other factors (see paragraphs 6.44–6.86).

6.44   In most cases, no single factor will determine which measurement basis should be selected. The relative importance of each factor will depend on facts and circumstances.

6.45   The information provided by a measurement basis must be useful to users of financial statements. To achieve this, the information must be relevant and it must faithfully represent what it purports to represent. In addition, the information provided should be, as far as possible, comparable, verifiable, timely and understandable.

6.46   As explained in paragraph 2.21, the most efficient and effective process for applying the fundamental qualitative characteristics would usually be to identify the most relevant information about an economic phenomenon. If that information is not available or cannot be provided in a way that faithfully represents the economic phenomenon, the next most relevant type of information is considered. Paragraphs 6.49–6.76 provide further discussion of the role played by the qualitative characteristics in the selection of a measurement basis.

6.47   The discussion in paragraphs 6.49–6.76 focuses on the factors to be considered in selecting a measurement basis for recognised assets and recognised liabilities. Some of that discussion may also apply in selecting a measurement basis for information provided in the notes, for recognised or unrecognised items.

6.48   Paragraphs 6.77–6.82 discuss additional factors to consider in selecting a measurement basis on initial recognition. If the initial measurement basis is inconsistent with the subsequent measurement basis, income and expenses might be recognised at the time of the first subsequent measurement solely because of the change in measurement basis. Recognising such income and expenses might appear to depict a transaction or other event when, in fact, no such transaction or event has occurred. Hence, the choice of measurement basis for an asset or liability, and for the related income and expenses, is determined by considering both initial measurement and subsequent measurement.

Relevance

6.49   The relevance of information provided by a measurement basis for an asset or liability and for the related income and expenses is affected by:

(a)   the characteristics of the asset or liability (see paragraphs 6.50–6.53); and

(b)   how that asset or liability contributes to future cash flows (see paragraphs 6.54–6.57).

Characteristics of the asset or liability

6.50   The relevance of information provided by a measurement basis depends partly on the characteristics of the asset or liability, in particular, on the variability of cash flows and on whether the value of the asset or liability is sensitive to market factors or other risks.

6.51   If the value of an asset or liability is sensitive to market factors or other risks, its historical cost might differ significantly from its current value. Consequently, historical cost may not provide relevant information if information about changes in value is important to users of financial statements. For example, amortised cost cannot provide relevant information about a financial asset or financial liability that is a derivative.

6.52   Furthermore, if historical cost is used, changes in value are reported not when that value changes, but when an event such as disposal, impairment or fulfilment occurs. This could be incorrectly interpreted as implying that all the income and expenses recognised at the time of that event arose then, rather than over the periods during which the asset or liability was held. Moreover, because measurement at historical cost does not provide timely information about changes in value, income and expenses reported on that basis may lack predictive value and confirmatory value by not depicting the full effect of the entity's exposure to risk arising from holding the asset or liability during the reporting period.

6.53   Changes in the fair value of an asset or liability reflect changes in expectations of market participants and changes in their risk preferences. Depending on the characteristics of the asset or liability being measured and on the nature of the entity's business activities, information reflecting those changes may not always provide predictive value or confirmatory value to users of financial statements. This may be the case when the entity's business activities do not involve selling the asset or transferring the liability, for example, if the entity holds assets solely for use or solely for collecting contractual cash flows or if the entity is to fulfil liabilities itself.

Contribution to future cash flows

6.54   As noted in paragraph 1.14, some economic resources produce cash flows directly; in other cases, economic resources are used in combination to produce cash flows indirectly. How economic resources are used, and hence how assets and liabilities produce cash flows, depends in part on the nature of the business activities conducted by the entity.

6.55   When a business activity of an entity involves the use of several economic resources that produce cash flows indirectly, by being used in combination to produce and market goods or services to customers, historical cost or current cost is likely to provide relevant information about that activity. For example, property, plant and equipment is typically used in combination with an entity's other economic resources. Similarly, inventory typically cannot be sold to a customer, except by making extensive use of the entity's other economic resources (for example, in production and marketing activities). Paragraphs 6.24–6.31 and 6.40–6.42 explain how measuring such assets at historical cost or current cost can provide relevant information that can be used to derive margins achieved during the period.

6.56   For assets and liabilities that produce cash flows directly, such as assets that can be sold independently and without a significant economic penalty (for example, without significant business disruption), the measurement basis that provides the most relevant information is likely to be a current value that incorporates current estimates of the amount, timing and uncertainty of the future cash flows.

6.57   When a business activity of an entity involves managing financial assets and financial liabilities with the objective of collecting contractual cash flows, amortised cost may provide relevant information that can be used to derive the margin between the interest earned on the assets and the interest incurred on the liabilities. However, in assessing whether amortised cost will provide useful information, it is also necessary to consider the characteristics of the financial asset or financial liability. Amortised cost is unlikely to provide relevant information about cash flows that depend on factors other than principal and interest.

Faithful representation

6.58   When assets and liabilities are related in some way, using different measurement bases for those assets and liabilities can create a measurement inconsistency (accounting mismatch). If financial statements contain measurement inconsistencies, those financial statements may not faithfully represent some aspects of the entity's financial position and financial performance. Consequently, in some circumstances, using the same measurement basis for related assets and liabilities may provide users of financial statements with information that is more useful than the information that would result from using different measurement bases. This may be particularly likely when the cash flows from one asset or liability are directly linked to the cash flows from another asset or liability.

6.59   As noted in paragraphs 2.13 and 2.18, although a perfectly faithful representation is free from error, this does not mean that measures must be perfectly accurate in all respects.

6.60   When a measure cannot be determined directly by observing prices in an active market and must instead be estimated, measurement uncertainty arises. The level of measurement uncertainty associated with a particular measurement basis may affect whether information provided by that measurement basis provides a faithful representation of an entity's financial position and financial performance. A high level of measurement uncertainty does not necessarily prevent the use of a measurement basis that provides relevant information. However, in some cases the level of measurement uncertainty is so high that information provided by a measurement basis might not provide a sufficiently faithful representation (see paragraph 2.22). In such cases, it is appropriate to consider selecting a different measurement basis that would also result in relevant information.

6.61   Measurement uncertainty is different from both outcome uncertainty and existence uncertainty:

(a)   outcome uncertainty arises when there is uncertainty about the amount or timing of any inflow or outflow of economic benefits that will result from an asset or liability.

(b)   existence uncertainty arises when it is uncertain whether an asset or a liability exists. Paragraphs 5.12–5.14 discuss how existence uncertainty may affect decisions about whether an entity recognises an asset or liability when it is uncertain whether that asset or liability exists.

6.62 The presence of outcome uncertainty or existence uncertainty may sometimes contribute to measurement uncertainty. However, outcome uncertainty or existence uncertainty does not necessarily result in measurement uncertainty. For example, if the fair value of an asset can be determined directly by observing prices in an active market, no measurement uncertainty is associated with the measurement of that fair value, even if it is uncertain how much cash the asset will ultimately produce and hence there is outcome uncertainty.

Enhancing qualitative characteristics and the cost constraint

6.63 The enhancing qualitative characteristics of comparability, understandability and verifiability, and the cost constraint, have implications for the selection of a measurement basis. The following paragraphs discuss those implications. Paragraphs 6.69–6.76 discuss further implications specific to particular measurement bases. The enhancing qualitative characteristic of timeliness has no specific implications for measurement.

6.64 Just as cost constrains other financial reporting decisions, it also constrains the selection of a measurement basis. Hence, in selecting a measurement basis, it is important to consider whether the benefits of the information provided to users of financial statements by that measurement basis are likely to justify the costs of providing and using that information.

6.65 Consistently using the same measurement bases for the same items, either from period to period within a reporting entity or in a single period across entities, can help make financial statements more comparable.

6.66 A change in measurement basis can make financial statements less understandable. However, a change may be justified if other factors outweigh the reduction in understandability, for example, if the change results in more relevant information. If a change is made, users of financial statements may need explanatory information to enable them to understand the effect of that change.

6.67 Understandability depends partly on how many different measurement bases are used and on whether they change over time. In general, if more measurement bases are used in a set of financial statements, the resulting information becomes more complex and, hence, less understandable and the totals or subtotals in the statement of financial position and the statement(s) of financial performance become less informative. However, it could be appropriate to use more measurement bases if that is necessary to provide useful information.

6.68 Verifiability is enhanced by using measurement bases that result in measures that can be independently corroborated either directly, for example, by observing prices, or indirectly, for example, by checking inputs to a model. If a measure cannot be verified, users of financial statements may need explanatory information to enable them to understand how the measure was determined. In some such cases, it may be necessary to specify the use of a different measurement basis.

Historical cost

6.69   In many situations, it is simpler, and hence less costly, to measure historical cost than it is to measure a current value. In addition, measures determined applying a historical cost measurement basis are generally well understood and, in many cases, verifiable.

6.70   However, estimating consumption and identifying and measuring impairment losses or onerous liabilities can be subjective. Hence, the historical cost of an asset or liability can sometimes be as difficult to measure or verify as a current value.

6.71   Using a historical cost measurement basis, identical assets acquired, or liabilities incurred, at different times can be reported in the financial statements at different amounts. This can reduce comparability, both from period to period for a reporting entity and in a single period across entities.

Current value

6.72   Because fair value is determined from the perspective of market participants, not from an entity-specific perspective, and is independent of when the asset was acquired or the liability was incurred, identical assets or liabilities measured at fair value will, in principle, be measured at the same amount by entities that have access to the same markets. This can enhance comparability both from period to period for a reporting entity and in a single period across entities. In contrast, because value in use and fulfilment value reflect an entity-specific perspective, those measures could differ for identical assets or liabilities in different entities. Those differences may reduce comparability, particularly if the assets or liabilities contribute to cash flows in a similar manner.

6.73   If the fair value of an asset or liability can be determined directly by observing prices in an active market, the process of fair value measurement is low-cost, simple and easy to understand; and the fair value can be verified through direct observation.

6.74   Valuation techniques, sometimes including the use of cash-flow-based measurement techniques, may be needed to estimate fair value when it cannot be observed directly in an active market and are generally needed when determining value in use and fulfilment value. Depending on the techniques used:

(a)   estimating inputs to the valuation and applying the valuation technique may be costly and complex.

(b)   the inputs into the process may be subjective and it may be difficult to verify both the inputs and the validity of the process itself. Consequently, the measures of identical assets or liabilities may differ. That would reduce comparability.

6.75   In many cases, value in use cannot be determined meaningfully for an individual asset used in combination with other assets. Instead, the value in use is determined for a group of assets and the result may then need to be allocated to individual assets. This process can be subjective and arbitrary. In addition, estimates of value in use for an asset may inadvertently reflect the effect of synergies with other assets in the group. Hence, determining the value in use of an asset used in combination with other assets can be a costly process and its complexity and subjectivity reduces verifiability. For these reasons, value in use may not be a practical measurement basis for regular remeasurements of such assets. However, it may be useful for occasional remeasurements of assets, for example, when it is used in an impairment test to determine whether historical cost is fully recoverable.

6.76   Using a current cost measurement basis, identical assets acquired or liabilities incurred at different times are reported in the financial statements at the same amount. This can enhance comparability, both from period to period for a reporting entity and in a single period across entities. However, determining current cost can be complex, subjective and costly. For example, as noted in paragraph 6.22, it may be necessary to estimate the current cost of an asset by adjusting the current price of a new asset to reflect the current age and condition of the asset held by the entity. In addition, because of changes in technology and changes in business practices, many assets would not be replaced with identical assets. Thus, a further subjective adjustment to the current price of a new asset would be required in order to estimate the current cost of an asset equivalent to the existing asset. Also, splitting changes in current cost carrying amounts between the current cost of consumption and the effect of changes in prices (see paragraph 6.42) may be complex and require arbitrary assumptions. Because of these difficulties, current cost measures may lack verifiability and understandability.

Factors specific to initial measurement

6.77   Paragraphs 6.43–6.76 discuss factors to consider when selecting a measurement basis, whether for initial recognition or subsequent measurement. Paragraphs 6.78–6.82 discuss some additional factors to consider at initial recognition.

6.78   At initial recognition, the cost of an asset acquired, or of a liability incurred, as a result of an event that is a transaction on market terms is normally similar to its fair value at that date, unless transaction costs are significant. Nevertheless, even if those two amounts are similar, it is necessary to describe what measurement basis is used at initial recognition. If historical cost will be used subsequently, that measurement basis is also normally appropriate at initial recognition. Similarly, if a current value will be used subsequently, it is also normally appropriate at initial recognition. Using the same measurement basis for initial recognition and subsequent measurement avoids recognising income or expenses at the time of the first subsequent measurement solely because of a change in measurement basis (see paragraph 6.48).

6.79   When an entity acquires an asset, or incurs a liability, in exchange for transferring another asset or liability as a result of a transaction on market terms, the initial measure of the asset acquired, or the liability incurred, determines whether any income or expenses arise from the transaction. When an asset or liability is measured at cost, no income or expenses arise at initial recognition, unless income or expenses arise from the derecognition of the transferred asset or liability, or unless the asset is impaired or the liability is onerous.

6.80   Assets may be acquired, or liabilities may be incurred, as a result of an event that is not a transaction on market terms. For example:

(a)   the transaction price may be affected by relationships between the parties, or by financial distress or other duress of one of the parties;

(b)   an asset may be granted to the entity free of charge by a government or donated to the entity by another party;

(c)   a liability may be imposed by legislation or regulation; or

(d)   a liability to pay compensation or a penalty may arise from an act of wrongdoing.

6.81   In such cases, measuring the asset acquired, or the liability incurred, at its historical cost may not provide a faithful representation of the entity's assets and liabilities and of any income or expenses arising from the transaction or other event. Hence, it may be appropriate to measure the asset acquired, or the liability incurred, at deemed cost, as described in paragraph 6.6. Any difference between that deemed cost and any consideration given or received would be recognised as income or expenses at initial recognition.

6.82   When assets are acquired, or liabilities incurred, as a result of an event that is not a transaction on market terms, all relevant aspects of the transaction or other event need to be identified and considered. For example, it may be necessary to recognise other assets, other liabilities, contributions from holders of equity claims or distributions to holders of equity claims to faithfully represent the substance of the effect of the transaction or other event on the entity's financial position (see paragraphs 4.59–4.62) and any related effect on the entity's financial performance.

More than one measurement basis

6.83   Sometimes, consideration of the factors described in paragraphs 6.43–6.76 may lead to the conclusion that more than one measurement basis is needed for an asset or liability and for related income and expenses in order to provide relevant information that faithfully represents both the entity's financial position and its financial performance.

6.84   In most cases, the most understandable way to provide that information is:

(a)   to use a single measurement basis both for the asset or liability in the statement of financial position and for related income and expenses in the statement(s) of financial performance; and

(b)   to provide in the notes additional information applying a different measurement basis.

6.85   However, in some cases, that information is more relevant, or results in a more faithful representation of both the entity's financial position and its financial performance, through the use of:

(a)   a current value measurement basis for the asset or liability in the statement of financial position; and

(b)   a different measurement basis for the related income and expenses in the statement of profit or loss[10] (see paragraphs 7.17–7.18).

In selecting those measurement bases, it is necessary to consider the factors discussed in paragraphs 6.43–6.76.

6.86   In such cases, the total income or total expenses arising in the period from the change in the current value of the asset or liability is separated and classified (see paragraphs 7.14–7.19) so that:

(a)   the statement of profit or loss includes the income or expenses measured applying the measurement basis selected for that statement; and

(b)   other comprehensive income includes all the remaining income or expenses. As a result, the accumulated other comprehensive income related to that asset or liability equals the difference between:

    (i)   the carrying amount of the asset or liability in the statement of financial position; and

    (ii)   the carrying amount that would have been determined applying the measurement basis selected for the statement of profit or loss.

Measurement of equity

6.87   The total carrying amount of equity (total equity) is not measured directly. It equals the total of the carrying amounts of all recognised assets less the total of the carrying amounts of all recognised liabilities.

6.88   Because general purpose financial statements are not designed to show an entity's value, the total carrying amount of equity will not generally equal:

(a)   the aggregate market value of equity claims on the entity;

(b)   the amount that could be raised by selling the entity as a whole on a going concern basis; or

(c)   the amount that could be raised by selling all of the entity's assets and settling all of its liabilities.

6.89   Although total equity is not measured directly, it may be appropriate to measure directly the carrying amount of some individual classes of equity (see paragraph 4.65) and some components of equity (see paragraph 4.66). Nevertheless, because total equity is measured as a residual, at least one class of equity cannot be measured directly. Similarly, at least one component of equity cannot be measured directly.

---

10 The *Conceptual Framework* does not specify whether the statement(s) of financial performance comprise(s) a single statement or two statements. The *Conceptual Framework* uses the term 'statement of profit or loss' to refer both to a separate statement and to a separate section within a single statement of financial performance.

6.90   The total carrying amount of an individual class of equity or component of equity is normally positive, but can be negative in some circumstances. Similarly, total equity is generally positive, but it can be negative, depending on which assets and liabilities are recognised and on how they are measured.

Cash-flow-based measurement techniques

6.91   Sometimes, a measure cannot be observed directly. In some such cases, one way to estimate the measure is by using cash-flow-based measurement techniques. Such techniques are not measurement bases. They are techniques used in applying a measurement basis. Hence, when using such a technique, it is necessary to identify which measurement basis is used and the extent to which the technique reflects the factors applicable to that measurement basis. For example, if the measurement basis is fair value, the applicable factors are those described in paragraph 6.14.

6.92   Cash-flow-based measurement techniques can be used in applying a modified measurement basis, for example, fulfilment value modified to exclude the effect of the possibility that the entity may fail to fulfil a liability (own credit risk). Modifying measurement bases may sometimes result in information that is more relevant to the users of financial statements or that may be less costly to produce or to understand. However, modified measurement bases may also be more difficult for users of financial statements to understand.

6.93   Outcome uncertainty (see paragraph 6.61(a)) arises from uncertainties about the amount or timing of future cash flows. Those uncertainties are important characteristics of assets and liabilities. When measuring an asset or liability by reference to estimates of uncertain future cash flows, one factor to consider is possible variations in the estimated amount or timing of those cash flows (see paragraph 6.14(b)). Those variations are considered in selecting a single amount from within the range of possible cash flows. The amount selected is itself sometimes the amount of a possible outcome, but this is not always the case. The amount that provides the most relevant information is usually one from within the central part of the range (a central estimate). Different central estimates provide different information. For example:

(a)   the expected value (the probability-weighted average, also known as the statistical mean) reflects the entire range of outcomes and gives more weight to the outcomes that are more likely. The expected value is not intended to predict the ultimate inflow or outflow of cash or other economic benefits arising from that asset or liability.

(b)   the maximum amount that is more likely than not to occur (similar to the statistical median) indicates that the probability of a subsequent loss is no more than 50% and that the probability of a subsequent gain is no more than 50%.

(c)   the most likely outcome (the statistical mode) is the single most likely ultimate inflow or outflow arising from an asset or liability.

6.94   A central estimate depends on estimates of future cash flows and possible variations in their amounts or timing. It does not capture the price for bearing the uncertainty that the ultimate outcome may differ from that central estimate (that is, the factor described in paragraph 6.14(d)).

6.95   No central estimate gives complete information about the range of possible outcomes. Hence users may need information about the range of possible outcomes.

Conceptual Framework

Contents

Presentation and disclosure as communication tools

7.1   A reporting entity communicates information about its assets, liabilities, equity, income and expenses by presenting and disclosing information in its financial statements.

7.2   Effective communication of information in financial statements makes that information more relevant and contributes to a faithful representation of an entity's assets, liabilities, equity, income and expenses. It also enhances the understandability and comparability of information in financial statements. Effective communication of information in financial statements requires:

         (a)   focusing on presentation and disclosure objectives and principles rather than focusing on rules;

         (b)   classifying information in a manner that groups similar items and separates dissimilar items; and

         (c)   aggregating information in such a way that it is not obscured either by unnecessary detail or by excessive aggregation.

7.3   Just as cost constrains other financial reporting decisions, it also constrains decisions about presentation and disclosure. Hence, in making decisions about presentation and disclosure, it is important to consider whether the benefits provided to users of financial statements by presenting or disclosing particular information are likely to justify the costs of providing and using that information.

Presentation and disclosure objectives and principles

7.4   To facilitate effective communication of information in financial statements, when developing presentation and disclosure requirements in Standards a balance is needed between:

         (a)   giving entities the flexibility to provide relevant information that faithfully represents the entity's assets, liabilities, equity, income and expenses; and

         (b)   requiring information that is comparable, both from period to period for a reporting entity and in a single reporting period across entities.

7.5   Including presentation and disclosure objectives in Standards supports effective communication in financial statements because such objectives help entities to identify useful information and to decide how to communicate that information in the most effective manner.

7.6   Effective communication in financial statements is also supported by considering the following principles:

         (a)   entity-specific information is more useful than standardised descriptions, sometimes referred to as 'boilerplate'; and

   (b)   duplication of information in different parts of the financial statements is usually unnecessary and can make financial statements less understandable.

Classification

7.7   Classification is the sorting of assets, liabilities, equity, income or expenses on the basis of shared characteristics for presentation and disclosure purposes. Such characteristics include—but are not limited to—the nature of the item, its role (or function) within the business activities conducted by the entity, and how it is measured.

7.8   Classifying dissimilar assets, liabilities, equity, income or expenses together can obscure relevant information, reduce understandability and comparability and may not provide a faithful representation of what it purports to represent.

Classification of assets and liabilities

7.9   Classification is applied to the unit of account selected for an asset or liability (see paragraphs 4.48–4.55). However, it may sometimes be appropriate to separate an asset or liability into components that have different characteristics and to classify those components separately. That would be appropriate when classifying those components separately would enhance the usefulness of the resulting financial information. For example, it could be appropriate to separate an asset or liability into current and non-current components and to classify those components separately.

Offsetting

7.10   Offsetting occurs when an entity recognises and measures both an asset and liability as separate units of account, but groups them into a single net amount in the statement of financial position. Offsetting classifies dissimilar items together and therefore is generally not appropriate.

7.11   Offsetting assets and liabilities differs from treating a set of rights and obligations as a single unit of account (see paragraphs 4.48–4.55).

Classification of equity

7.12   To provide useful information, it may be necessary to classify equity claims separately if those equity claims have different characteristics (see paragraph 4.65).

7.13   Similarly, to provide useful information, it may be necessary to classify components of equity separately if some of those components are subject to particular legal, regulatory or other requirements. For example, in some jurisdictions, an entity is permitted to make distributions to holders of equity claims only if the entity has sufficient reserves specified as distributable (see paragraph 4.66). Separate presentation or disclosure of those reserves may provide useful information.

Classification of income and expenses

7.14   Classification is applied to:

(a)   income and expenses resulting from the unit of account selected for an asset or liability; or

(b)   components of such income and expenses if those components have different characteristics and are identified separately. For example, a change in the current value of an asset can include the effects of value changes and the accrual of interest (see Table 6.1). It would be appropriate to classify those components separately if doing so would enhance the usefulness of the resulting financial information.

Profit or loss and other comprehensive income

7.15   Income and expenses are classified and included either:

(a)   in the statement of profit or loss;[11] or

(b)   outside the statement of profit or loss, in other comprehensive income.

7.16   The statement of profit or loss is the primary source of information about an entity's financial performance for the reporting period. That statement contains a total for profit or loss that provides a highly summarised depiction of the entity's financial performance for the period. Many users of financial statements incorporate that total in their analysis either as a starting point for that analysis or as the main indicator of the entity's financial performance for the period. Nevertheless, understanding an entity's financial performance for the period requires an analysis of all recognised income and expenses — including income and expenses included in other comprehensive income — as well as an analysis of other information included in the financial statements.

7.17   Because the statement of profit or loss is the primary source of information about an entity's financial performance for the period, all income and expenses are, in principle, included in that statement. However, in developing Standards, the Board may decide in exceptional circumstances that income or expenses arising from a change in the current value of an asset or liability are to be included in other comprehensive income when doing so would result in the statement of profit or loss providing more relevant information, or providing a more faithful representation of the entity's financial performance for that period.

7.18   Income and expenses that arise on a historical cost measurement basis (see Table 6.1) are included in the statement of profit or loss. That is also the case when income and expenses of that type are separately identified as a component of a change in the current value of an asset or liability. For example, if a financial asset is measured at current value and if interest

---

11 The *Conceptual Framework* does not specify whether the statement(s) of financial performance comprise(s) a single statement or two statements. The *Conceptual Framework* uses the term 'statement of profit or loss' to refer to a separate statement and to a separate section within a single statement of financial performance. Likewise, it uses the term 'total for profit or loss' to refer both to a total for a separate statement and to a subtotal for a section within a single statement of financial performance.

income is identified separately from other changes in value, that interest income is included in the statement of profit or loss.

7.19 In principle, income and expenses included in other comprehensive income in one period are reclassified from other comprehensive income into the statement of profit or loss in a future period when doing so results in the statement of profit or loss providing more relevant information, or providing a more faithful representation of the entity's financial performance for that future period. However, if, for example, there is no clear basis for identifying the period in which reclassification would have that result, or the amount that should be reclassified, the Board may, in developing Standards, decide that income and expenses included in other comprehensive income are not to be subsequently reclassified.

Aggregation

7.20 Aggregation is the adding together of assets, liabilities, equity, income or expenses that have shared characteristics and are included in the same classification.

7.21 Aggregation makes information more useful by summarising a large volume of detail. However, aggregation conceals some of that detail. Hence, a balance needs to be found so that relevant information is not obscured either by a large amount of insignificant detail or by excessive aggregation.

7.22 Different levels of aggregation may be needed in different parts of the financial statements. For example, typically, the statement of financial position and the statement(s) of financial performance provide summarised information and more detailed information is provided in the notes.

CONTENTS

> *The material included in Chapter 8 has been carried forward unchanged from the* Conceptual Framework for Financial Reporting *issued in 2010. That material originally appeared in the* Framework for the Preparation and Presentation of Financial Statements *issued in 1989.*

Concepts of capital

8.1   A financial concept of capital is adopted by most entities in preparing their financial statements. Under a financial concept of capital, such as invested money or invested purchasing power, capital is synonymous with the net assets or equity of the entity. Under a physical concept of capital, such as operating capability, capital is regarded as the productive capacity of the entity based on, for example, units of output per day.

8.2   The selection of the appropriate concept of capital by an entity should be based on the needs of the users of its financial statements. Thus, a financial concept of capital should be adopted if the users of financial statements are primarily concerned with the maintenance of nominal invested capital or the purchasing power of invested capital. If, however, the main concern of users is with the operating capability of the entity, a physical concept of capital should be used. The concept chosen indicates the goal to be attained in determining profit, even though there may be some measurement difficulties in making the concept operational.

Concepts of capital maintenance and the determination of profit

8.3   The concepts of capital in paragraph 8.1 give rise to the following concepts of capital maintenance:

(a)   *Financial capital maintenance.* Under this concept a profit is earned only if the financial (or money) amount of the net assets at the end of the period exceeds the financial (or money) amount of net assets at the beginning of the period, after excluding any distributions to, and contributions from, owners during the period. Financial capital maintenance can be measured in either nominal monetary units or units of constant purchasing power.

(b)   *Physical capital maintenance.* Under this concept a profit is earned only if the physical productive capacity (or operating capability) of the entity (or the resources or funds needed to achieve that capacity) at the end of the period exceeds the physical productive capacity at the beginning of the period, after excluding any distributions to, and contributions from, owners during the period.

8.4   The concept of capital maintenance is concerned with how an entity defines the capital that it seeks to maintain. It provides the linkage between the concepts of capital and the concepts of profit because it provides the point of reference by which profit is measured; it is a prerequisite for distinguishing between an entity's return on capital and its return of capital; only inflows of assets in excess of amounts needed to maintain capital may be regarded as profit and therefore as a return on capital. Hence, profit is the residual amount that remains after expenses (including capital maintenance adjustments, where appropriate) have been deducted from income. If expenses exceed income the residual amount is a loss.

8.5   The physical capital maintenance concept requires the adoption of the current cost basis of measurement. The financial capital maintenance concept, however, does not require the use of a particular basis of measurement. Selection of the basis under this concept is dependent on the type of financial capital that the entity is seeking to maintain.

8.6   The principal difference between the two concepts of capital maintenance is the treatment of the effects of changes in the prices of assets and liabilities of the entity. In general terms, an entity has maintained its capital if it has as much capital at the end of the period as it had at the beginning of the period. Any amount over and above that required to maintain the capital at the beginning of the period is profit.

8.7   Under the concept of financial capital maintenance where capital is defined in terms of nominal monetary units, profit represents the increase in nominal money capital over the period. Thus, increases in the prices of assets held over the period, conventionally referred to as holding gains, are, conceptually, profits. They may not be recognised as such, however, until the assets are disposed of in an exchange transaction. When the concept of financial capital maintenance is defined in terms of constant purchasing power units, profit represents the increase in invested purchasing power over the period. Thus, only that part of the increase in the prices of assets that exceeds the increase in the general level of prices is regarded as profit. The rest of the increase is treated as a capital maintenance adjustment and, hence, as part of equity.

8.8   Under the concept of physical capital maintenance when capital is defined in terms of the physical productive capacity, profit represents the increase in that capital over the period. All price changes affecting the assets and liabilities of the entity are viewed as changes in the measurement of the physical productive capacity of the entity; hence, they are treated as capital maintenance adjustments that are part of equity and not as profit.

8.9   The selection of the measurement bases and concept of capital maintenance will determine the accounting model used in the preparation of the financial statements. Different accounting models exhibit different degrees of relevance and reliability and, as in other areas, management must seek a balance between relevance and reliability. This *Conceptual Framework* is applicable to a range of accounting models and provides guidance on preparing and presenting the financial statements constructed under the chosen model. At the present time, it is not the intention of the Board to prescribe a particular model other than in exceptional circumstances, such as for those entities reporting in the currency of a hyperinflationary economy. This intention will, however, be reviewed in the light of world developments.

Capital maintenance adjustments

8.10   The revaluation or restatement of assets and liabilities gives rise to increases or decreases in equity. While these increases or decreases meet the definition of income and expenses, they are not included in the income statement under certain concepts of capital maintenance. Instead these items are included in equity as capital maintenance adjustments or revaluation reserves.

Appendix
Defined terms

The following defined terms are extracted or derived from the relevant paragraphs of the Conceptual
Framework for Financial Reporting.

aggregation	The adding together of assets, liabilities, equity, income or expenses that have shared characteristics and are included in the same classification.	CF.7.20
asset	A present economic resource controlled by the entity as a result of past events.	CF.4.3
carrying amount	The amount at which an asset, a liability or equity is recognised in the statement of financial position.	CF.5.1
classification	The sorting of assets, liabilities, equity, income or expenses on the basis of shared characteristics for presentation and disclosure purposes.	CF.7.7
combined financial statements	Financial statements of a reporting entity that comprises two or more entities that are not all linked by a parent-subsidiary relationship.	CF.3.12
consolidated financial statements	Financial statements of a reporting entity that comprises both the parent and its subsidiaries.	CF.3.11
control of an economic resource	The present ability to direct the use of the economic resource and obtain the economic benefits that may flow from it.	CF.4.20
derecognition	The removal of all or part of a recognised asset or liability from an entity's statement of financial position.	CF.5.26
economic resource	A right that has the potential to produce economic benefits.	CF.4.4
enhancing qualitative characteristic	A qualitative characteristic that makes useful information more useful. The enhancing qualitative characteristics are comparability, verifiability, timeliness and understandability.	CF.2.4, CF.2.23
equity	The residual interest in the assets of the entity after deducting all its liabilities.	CF.4.63
equity claim	A claim on the residual interest in the assets of the entity after deducting all its liabilities.	CF.4.64
executory contract	A contract, or a portion of a contract, that is equally unperformed – neither party has fulfilled any of its obligations, or both parties have partially fulfilled their obligations to an equal extent.	CF.4.56
existence uncertainty	Uncertainty about whether an asset or liability exists.	CF.4.13, CF.4.35

continued...

...continued

expenses	Decreases in assets, or increases in liabilities, that result in decreases in equity, other than those relating to distributions to holders of equity claims.	CF.4.69
fundamental qualitative characteristic	A qualitative characteristic that financial information must possess to be useful to the primary users of general purpose financial reports. The fundamental qualitative characteristics are relevance and faithful representation.	CF.2.4, CF.2.5
general purpose financial report	A report that provides financial information about the reporting entity's economic resources, claims against the entity and changes in those economic resources and claims that is useful to primary users in making decisions relating to providing resources to the entity.	CF.1.2, CF.1.12
general purpose financial statements	A particular form of general purpose financial reports that provide information about the reporting entity's assets, liabilities, equity, income and expenses.	CF.3.2
income	Increases in assets, or decreases in liabilities, that result in increases in equity, other than those relating to contributions from holders of equity claims.	CF.4.68
liability	A present obligation of the entity to transfer an economic resource as a result of past events.	CF.4.26
material information	Information is material if omitting, misstating, or obscuring it could reasonably be expected to influence decisions that the primary users of general purpose financial reports make on the basis of those reports, which provide financial information about a specific reporting entity.	CF.2.11
measure	The result of applying a measurement basis to an asset or liability and related income and expenses.	CF.6.1
measurement basis	An identified feature—for example, historical cost, fair value or fulfilment value—of an item being measured.	CF.6.1
measurement uncertainty	Uncertainty that arises when monetary amounts in financial reports cannot be observed directly and must instead be estimated.	CF.2.19
offsetting	Grouping an asset and liability that are recognised and measured as separate units of account into a single net amount in the statement of financial position.	CF.7.10

continued...

...continued

outcome uncertainty	Uncertainty about the amount or timing of any inflow or outflow of economic benefits that will result from an asset or liability.	CF.6.61
potential to produce economic benefits	Within an economic resource, a feature that already exists and that, in at least one circumstance, would produce for the entity economic benefits beyond those available to all other parties.	CF.4.14
primary users (of general purpose financial reports)	Existing and potential investors, lenders and other creditors.	CF.1.2
prudence	The exercise of caution when making judgements under conditions of uncertainty. The exercise of prudence means that assets and income are not overstated and liabilities and expenses are not understated. Equally, the exercise of prudence does not allow for the understatement of assets or income or the overstatement of liabilities or expenses.	CF.2.16
recognition	The process of capturing for inclusion in the statement of financial position or the statement(s) of financial performance an item that meets the definition of one of the elements of financial statements — an asset, a liability, equity, income or expenses. Recognition involves depicting the item in one of those statements — either alone or in aggregation with other items — in words and by a monetary amount, and including that amount in one or more totals in that statement.	CF.5.1
reporting entity	An entity that is required, or chooses, to prepare general purpose financial statements.	CF.3.10
unconsolidated financial statements	Financial statements of a reporting entity that is the parent alone.	CF.3.11
unit of account	The right or the group of rights, the obligation or the group of obligations, or the group of rights and obligations, to which recognition criteria and measurement concepts are applied.	CF.4.48
useful financial information	Financial information that is useful to primary users of general purpose financial reports in making decisions relating to providing resources to the reporting entity. To be useful, financial information must be relevant and faithfully represent what it purports to represent.	CF.1.2, CF.2.4

continued...

...continued

users (of general purpose financial reports)	See primary users (of general purpose financial reports).	–

Approval by the Board of the *Conceptual Framework for Financial Reporting* issued in March 2018

The *Conceptual Framework for Financial Reporting* was approved for issue by 13 of the 14 members of the International Accounting Standards Board. Ms Tarca abstained in view of her recent appointment to the Board.

Hans Hoogervorst	Chairman
Suzanne Lloyd	Vice-Chair
Nick Anderson	
Martin Edelmann	
Françoise Flores	
Amaro Luiz De Oliveira Gomes	
Gary Kabureck	
Jianqiao Lu	
Takatsugu Ochi	
Darrel Scott	
Thomas Scott	
Chungwoo Suh	
Ann Tarca	
Mary Tokar	

IFRS 1

First-time Adoption of International Financial Reporting Standards

In April 2001 the International Accounting Standards Board (Board) adopted SIC-8 *First-time Application of IASs as the Primary Basis of Accounting*, which had been issued by the Standing Interpretations Committee of the International Accounting Standards Committee in July 1998.

In June 2003 the Board issued IFRS 1 *First-time Adoption of International Financial Reporting Standards* to replace SIC-8. IAS 1 *Presentation of Financial Statements* (as revised in 2007) amended the terminology used throughout IFRS Standards, including IFRS 1.

The Board restructured IFRS 1 in November 2008. In December 2010 the Board amended IFRS 1 to reflect that a first-time adopter would restate past transactions from the date of transition to IFRS Standards instead of at 1 January 2004.

Since it was issued in 2003, IFRS 1 was amended to accommodate first-time adoption requirements resulting from new or amended Standards. IFRS 1 was amended by *Government Loans* (issued March 2012), which added an exception to the retrospective application of IFRS to require that first time adopters apply the requirements in IFRS 9 *Financial Instruments* and IAS 20 *Accounting for Government Grants and Disclosure of Government Assistance* prospectively to government loans existing at the date of transition to IFRS.

Other Standards have made minor amendments to IFRS 1. They include *Improvements to IFRSs* (issued May 2010), Revised IFRS 3 *Business Combinations* (issued January 2008), *Severe Hyperinflation and Removal of Fixed Dates for First-time Adopters* (Amendments to IFRS 1) (issued December 2010), IFRS 10 *Consolidated Financial Statements* (issued May 2011), IFRS 11 *Joint Arrangements* (issued May 2011), IFRS 13 *Fair Value Measurement* (issued May 2011), IAS 19 *Employee Benefits* (issued June 2011), *Presentation of Items of Other Comprehensive Income* (Amendments to IAS 1) (issued June 2011), IFRIC 20 *Stripping Costs in the Production Phase of a Surface Mine* (issued October 2011), *Government Loans* (issued March 2012), *Annual Improvements to IFRSs 2009–2011 Cycle* (issued May 2012), *Consolidated Financial Statements, Joint Arrangements and Disclosure of Interests in Other Entities: Transition Guidance* (Amendments to IFRS 10, IFRS 11 and IFRS 12) (issued June 2012), *Investment Entities* (Amendments to IFRS 10, IFRS 12 and IAS 27) (issued October 2012), IFRS 9 *Financial Instruments* (Hedge Accounting and amendments to IFRS 9, IFRS 7 and IAS 39) (issued November 2013), IFRS 14 *Regulatory Deferral Accounts* (issued January 2014), *Accounting for Acquisitions of Interests in Joint Operations* (Amendments to IFRS 11) (issued May 2014), IFRS 15 *Revenue from Contracts with Customers* (issued May 2014), IFRS 9 *Financial Instruments* (issued July 2014), *Equity Method in Separate Financial Statements* (Amendments to IAS 27) (issued August 2014), IFRS 16 *Leases* (issued January 2016), *Annual Improvements to IFRS Standards 2014–2016 Cycle* (issued December 2016), which deleted several lapsed short-term exemptions, IFRIC 22 *Foreign Currency Transactions and Advance Consideration* (issued December 2016), IFRIC 23 *Uncertainty over Income Tax Treatments* (issued June 2017) and *Amendments to References to the Conceptual Framework in IFRS Standards* (issued March 2018).

CONTENTS

FOR THE ACCOMPANYING GUIDANCE LISTED BELOW, SEE PART B OF THIS EDITION

FOR THE BASIS FOR CONCLUSIONS, SEE PART C OF THIS EDITION

International Financial Reporting Standard 1 *First-time Adoption of International Financial Reporting Standards* (IFRS 1) is set out in paragraphs 1–40 and Appendices A–E. All the paragraphs have equal authority. Paragraphs in **bold type** state the main principles. Terms defined in Appendix A are in *italics* the first time they appear in the IFRS. Definitions of other terms are given in the Glossary for International Financial Reporting Standards. IFRS 1 should be read in the context of its objective and the Basis for Conclusions, the *Preface to IFRS Standards* and the *Conceptual Framework for Financial Reporting*. IAS 8 *Accounting Policies, Changes in Accounting Estimates and Errors* provides a basis for selecting and applying accounting policies in the absence of explicit guidance.

International Financial Reporting Standard 1
First-time Adoption of International Financial Reporting Standards

Objective

1 The objective of this IFRS is to ensure that an entity's *first IFRS financial statements*, and its interim financial reports for part of the period covered by those financial statements, contain high quality information that:

  (a) is transparent for users and comparable over all periods presented;

  (b) provides a suitable starting point for accounting in accordance with *International Financial Reporting Standards (IFRSs)*; and

  (c) can be generated at a cost that does not exceed the benefits.

Scope

2 An entity shall apply this IFRS in:

  (a) its first IFRS financial statements; and

  (b) each interim financial report, if any, that it presents in accordance with IAS 34 *Interim Financial Reporting* for part of the period covered by its first IFRS financial statements.

3 An entity's first IFRS financial statements are the first annual financial statements in which the entity adopts IFRSs, by an explicit and unreserved statement in those financial statements of compliance with IFRSs. Financial statements in accordance with IFRSs are an entity's first IFRS financial statements if, for example, the entity:

  (a) presented its most recent previous financial statements:

    (i) in accordance with national requirements that are not consistent with IFRSs in all respects;

    (ii) in conformity with IFRSs in all respects, except that the financial statements did not contain an explicit and unreserved statement that they complied with IFRSs;

    (iii) containing an explicit statement of compliance with some, but not all, IFRSs;

    (iv) in accordance with national requirements inconsistent with IFRSs, using some individual IFRSs to account for items for which national requirements did not exist; or

    (v) in accordance with national requirements, with a reconciliation of some amounts to the amounts determined in accordance with IFRSs;

(b)   prepared financial statements in accordance with IFRSs for internal use only, without making them available to the entity's owners or any other external users;

(c)   prepared a reporting package in accordance with IFRSs for consolidation purposes without preparing a complete set of financial statements as defined in IAS 1 *Presentation of Financial Statements* (as revised in 2007); or

(d)   did not present financial statements for previous periods.

4   This IFRS applies when an entity first adopts IFRSs. It does not apply when, for example, an entity:

(a)   stops presenting financial statements in accordance with national requirements, having previously presented them as well as another set of financial statements that contained an explicit and unreserved statement of compliance with IFRSs;

(b)   presented financial statements in the previous year in accordance with national requirements and those financial statements contained an explicit and unreserved statement of compliance with IFRSs; or

(c)   presented financial statements in the previous year that contained an explicit and unreserved statement of compliance with IFRSs, even if the auditors qualified their audit report on those financial statements.

4A   Notwithstanding the requirements in paragraphs 2 and 3, an entity that has applied IFRSs in a previous reporting period, but whose most recent previous annual financial statements did not contain an explicit and unreserved statement of compliance with IFRSs, must either apply this IFRS or else apply IFRSs retrospectively in accordance with IAS 8 *Accounting Policies, Changes in Accounting Estimates and Errors* as if the entity had never stopped applying IFRSs.

4B   When an entity does not elect to apply this IFRS in accordance with paragraph 4A, the entity shall nevertheless apply the disclosure requirements in paragraphs 23A–23B of IFRS 1, in addition to the disclosure requirements in IAS 8.

5   This IFRS does not apply to changes in accounting policies made by an entity that already applies IFRSs. Such changes are the subject of:

(a)   requirements on changes in accounting policies in IAS 8 *Accounting Policies, Changes in Accounting Estimates and Errors*; and

(b)   specific transitional requirements in other IFRSs.

Recognition and measurement

Opening IFRS statement of financial position

6   An entity shall prepare and present an *opening IFRS statement of financial position* at the *date of transition to IFRSs*. This is the starting point for its accounting in accordance with IFRSs.

Accounting policies

7   An entity shall use the same accounting policies in its opening IFRS statement of financial position and throughout all periods presented in its first IFRS financial statements. Those accounting policies shall comply with each IFRS effective at the end of its *first IFRS reporting period*, except as specified in paragraphs 13–19 and Appendices B–E.

8   An entity shall not apply different versions of IFRSs that were effective at earlier dates. An entity may apply a new IFRS that is not yet mandatory if that IFRS permits early application.

Example: Consistent application of latest version of IFRSs

Background

The end of entity A's first IFRS reporting period is 31 December 20X5. Entity A decides to present comparative information in those financial statements for one year only (see paragraph 21). Therefore, its date of transition to IFRSs is the beginning of business on 1 January 20X4 (or, equivalently, close of business on 31 December 20X3). Entity A presented financial statements in accordance with its *previous GAAP* annually to 31 December each year up to, and including, 31 December 20X4.

Application of requirements

Entity A is required to apply the IFRSs effective for periods ending on 31 December 20X5 in:

(a)   preparing and presenting its opening IFRS statement of financial position at 1 January 20X4; and

(b)   preparing and presenting its statement of financial position for 31 December 20X5 (including comparative amounts for 20X4), statement of comprehensive income, statement of changes in equity and statement of cash flows for the year to 31 December 20X5 (including comparative amounts for 20X4) and disclosures (including comparative information for 20X4).

If a new IFRS is not yet mandatory but permits early application, entity A is permitted, but not required, to apply that IFRS in its first IFRS financial statements.

---

9   The transitional provisions in other IFRSs apply to changes in accounting policies made by an entity that already uses IFRSs; they do not apply to a *first-time adopter*'s transition to IFRSs, except as specified in Appendices B–E.

10   Except as described in paragraphs 13–19 and Appendices B–E, an entity shall, in its opening IFRS statement of financial position:

(a)   recognise all assets and liabilities whose recognition is required by IFRSs;

(b)   not recognise items as assets or liabilities if IFRSs do not permit such recognition;

(c)   reclassify items that it recognised in accordance with previous GAAP as one type of asset, liability or component of equity, but are a different type of asset, liability or component of equity in accordance with IFRSs; and

(d)   apply IFRSs in measuring all recognised assets and liabilities.

11   The accounting policies that an entity uses in its opening IFRS statement of financial position may differ from those that it used for the same date using its previous GAAP. The resulting adjustments arise from events and transactions before the date of transition to IFRSs. Therefore, an entity shall recognise those adjustments directly in retained earnings (or, if appropriate, another category of equity) at the date of transition to IFRSs.

12   This IFRS establishes two categories of exceptions to the principle that an entity's opening IFRS statement of financial position shall comply with each IFRS:

(a)   paragraphs 14–17 and Appendix B prohibit retrospective application of some aspects of other IFRSs.

(b)   Appendices C–E grant exemptions from some requirements of other IFRSs.

Exceptions to the retrospective application of other IFRSs

13   This IFRS prohibits retrospective application of some aspects of other IFRSs. These exceptions are set out in paragraphs 14–17 and Appendix B.

Estimates

14   **An entity's estimates in accordance with IFRSs at the date of transition to IFRSs shall be consistent with estimates made for the same date in accordance with previous GAAP (after adjustments to reflect any difference in accounting policies), unless there is objective evidence that those estimates were in error.**

15   An entity may receive information after the date of transition to IFRSs about estimates that it had made under previous GAAP. In accordance with paragraph 14, an entity shall treat the receipt of that information in the same way as non-adjusting events after the reporting period in accordance with IAS 10 *Events after the Reporting Period*. For example, assume that an entity's date of transition to IFRSs is 1 January 20X4 and new information on 15 July 20X4 requires the revision of an estimate made in accordance with previous GAAP at 31 December 20X3. The entity shall not reflect that new information in its opening IFRS statement of financial position (unless the estimates need adjustment for any differences in accounting policies or there is objective evidence that the estimates were in error). Instead, the entity shall reflect that new information in profit or loss (or, if appropriate, other comprehensive income) for the year ended 31 December 20X4.

16　An entity may need to make estimates in accordance with IFRSs at the date of transition to IFRSs that were not required at that date under previous GAAP. To achieve consistency with IAS 10, those estimates in accordance with IFRSs shall reflect conditions that existed at the date of transition to IFRSs. In particular, estimates at the date of transition to IFRSs of market prices, interest rates or foreign exchange rates shall reflect market conditions at that date.

17　Paragraphs 14–16 apply to the opening IFRS statement of financial position. They also apply to a comparative period presented in an entity's first IFRS financial statements, in which case the references to the date of transition to IFRSs are replaced by references to the end of that comparative period.

Exemptions from other IFRSs

18　An entity may elect to use one or more of the exemptions contained in Appendices C–E. An entity shall not apply these exemptions by analogy to other items.

19　[Deleted]

Presentation and disclosure

20　This IFRS does not provide exemptions from the presentation and disclosure requirements in other IFRSs.

Comparative information

21　An entity's first IFRS financial statements shall include at least three statements of financial position, two statements of profit or loss and other comprehensive income, two separate statements of profit or loss (if presented), two statements of cash flows and two statements of changes in equity and related notes, including comparative information for all statements presented.

Non-IFRS comparative information and historical summaries

22　Some entities present historical summaries of selected data for periods before the first period for which they present full comparative information in accordance with IFRSs. This IFRS does not require such summaries to comply with the recognition and measurement requirements of IFRSs. Furthermore, some entities present comparative information in accordance with previous GAAP as well as the comparative information required by IAS 1. In any financial statements containing historical summaries or comparative information in accordance with previous GAAP, an entity shall:

(a)　label the previous GAAP information prominently as not being prepared in accordance with IFRSs; and

(b)　disclose the nature of the main adjustments that would make it comply with IFRSs. An entity need not quantify those adjustments.

Explanation of transition to IFRSs

23 An entity shall explain how the transition from previous GAAP to IFRSs affected its reported financial position, financial performance and cash flows.

23A An entity that has applied IFRSs in a previous period, as described in paragraph 4A, shall disclose:

(a) the reason it stopped applying IFRSs; and

(b) the reason it is resuming the application of IFRSs.

23B When an entity, in accordance with paragraph 4A, does not elect to apply IFRS 1, the entity shall explain the reasons for electing to apply IFRSs as if it had never stopped applying IFRSs.

Reconciliations

24 To comply with paragraph 23, an entity's first IFRS financial statements shall include:

(a) reconciliations of its equity reported in accordance with previous GAAP to its equity in accordance with IFRSs for both of the following dates:

(i) the date of transition to IFRSs; and

(ii) the end of the latest period presented in the entity's most recent annual financial statements in accordance with previous GAAP.

(b) a reconciliation to its total comprehensive income in accordance with IFRSs for the latest period in the entity's most recent annual financial statements. The starting point for that reconciliation shall be total comprehensive income in accordance with previous GAAP for the same period or, if an entity did not report such a total, profit or loss under previous GAAP.

(c) if the entity recognised or reversed any impairment losses for the first time in preparing its opening IFRS statement of financial position, the disclosures that IAS 36 *Impairment of Assets* would have required if the entity had recognised those impairment losses or reversals in the period beginning with the date of transition to IFRSs.

25 The reconciliations required by paragraph 24(a) and (b) shall give sufficient detail to enable users to understand the material adjustments to the statement of financial position and statement of comprehensive income. If an entity presented a statement of cash flows under its previous GAAP, it shall also explain the material adjustments to the statement of cash flows.

26 If an entity becomes aware of errors made under previous GAAP, the reconciliations required by paragraph 24(a) and (b) shall distinguish the correction of those errors from changes in accounting policies.

27   IAS 8 does not apply to the changes in accounting policies an entity makes when it adopts IFRSs or to changes in those policies until after it presents its first IFRS financial statements. Therefore, IAS 8's requirements about changes in accounting policies do not apply in an entity's first IFRS financial statements.

27A   If during the period covered by its first IFRS financial statements an entity changes its accounting policies or its use of the exemptions contained in this IFRS, it shall explain the changes between its first IFRS interim financial report and its first IFRS financial statements, in accordance with paragraph 23, and it shall update the reconciliations required by paragraph 24(a) and (b).

28   If an entity did not present financial statements for previous periods, its first IFRS financial statements shall disclose that fact.

Designation of financial assets or financial liabilities

29   An entity is permitted to designate a previously recognised financial asset as a financial asset measured at fair value through profit or loss in accordance with paragraph D19A. The entity shall disclose the fair value of financial assets so designated at the date of designation and their classification and carrying amount in the previous financial statements.

29A   An entity is permitted to designate a previously recognised financial liability as a financial liability at fair value through profit or loss in accordance with paragraph D19. The entity shall disclose the fair value of financial liabilities so designated at the date of designation and their classification and carrying amount in the previous financial statements.

Use of fair value as deemed cost

30   If an entity uses fair value in its opening IFRS statement of financial position as *deemed cost* for an item of property, plant and equipment, an investment property, an intangible asset or a right-of-use asset (see paragraphs D5 and D7), the entity's first IFRS financial statements shall disclose, for each line item in the opening IFRS statement of financial position:

(a)   the aggregate of those fair values; and

(b)   the aggregate adjustment to the carrying amounts reported under previous GAAP.

Use of deemed cost for investments in subsidiaries, joint ventures and associates

31   Similarly, if an entity uses a deemed cost in its opening IFRS statement of financial position for an investment in a subsidiary, joint venture or associate in its separate financial statements (see paragraph D15), the entity's first IFRS separate financial statements shall disclose:

(a)   the aggregate deemed cost of those investments for which deemed cost is their previous GAAP carrying amount;

(b)   the aggregate deemed cost of those investments for which deemed cost is fair value; and

(c)   the aggregate adjustment to the carrying amounts reported under previous GAAP.

Use of deemed cost for oil and gas assets

31A   If an entity uses the exemption in paragraph D8A(b) for oil and gas assets, it shall disclose that fact and the basis on which carrying amounts determined under previous GAAP were allocated.

Use of deemed cost for operations subject to rate regulation

31B   If an entity uses the exemption in paragraph D8B for operations subject to rate regulation, it shall disclose that fact and the basis on which carrying amounts were determined under previous GAAP.

Use of deemed cost after severe hyperinflation

31C   If an entity elects to measure assets and liabilities at fair value and to use that fair value as the deemed cost in its opening IFRS statement of financial position because of severe hyperinflation (see paragraphs D26–D30), the entity's first IFRS financial statements shall disclose an explanation of how, and why, the entity had, and then ceased to have, a functional currency that has both of the following characteristics:

(a)   a reliable general price index is not available to all entities with transactions and balances in the currency.

(b)   exchangeability between the currency and a relatively stable foreign currency does not exist.

Interim financial reports

32   To comply with paragraph 23, if an entity presents an interim financial report in accordance with IAS 34 for part of the period covered by its first IFRS financial statements, the entity shall satisfy the following requirements in addition to the requirements of IAS 34:

(a)   Each such interim financial report shall, if the entity presented an interim financial report for the comparable interim period of the immediately preceding financial year, include:

(i)   a reconciliation of its equity in accordance with previous GAAP at the end of that comparable interim period to its equity under IFRSs at that date; and

(ii)   a reconciliation to its total comprehensive income in accordance with IFRSs for that comparable interim period (current and year to date). The starting point for that reconciliation shall be total comprehensive income in accordance with previous GAAP for that period or, if an entity did not report such a total, profit or loss in accordance with previous GAAP.

(b)　　In addition to the reconciliations required by (a), an entity's first interim financial report in accordance with IAS 34 for part of the period covered by its first IFRS financial statements shall include the reconciliations described in paragraph 24(a) and (b) (supplemented by the details required by paragraphs 25 and 26) or a cross-reference to another published document that includes these reconciliations.

(c)　　If an entity changes its accounting policies or its use of the exemptions contained in this IFRS, it shall explain the changes in each such interim financial report in accordance with paragraph 23 and update the reconciliations required by (a) and (b).

33　　IAS 34 requires minimum disclosures, which are based on the assumption that users of the interim financial report also have access to the most recent annual financial statements. However, IAS 34 also requires an entity to disclose 'any events or transactions that are material to an understanding of the current interim period'. Therefore, if a first-time adopter did not, in its most recent annual financial statements in accordance with previous GAAP, disclose information material to an understanding of the current interim period, its interim financial report shall disclose that information or include a cross-reference to another published document that includes it.

Effective date

34　　An entity shall apply this IFRS if its first IFRS financial statements are for a period beginning on or after 1 July 2009. Earlier application is permitted.

35　　An entity shall apply the amendments in paragraphs D1(n) and D23 for annual periods beginning on or after 1 July 2009. If an entity applies IAS 23 *Borrowing Costs* (as revised in 2007) for an earlier period, those amendments shall be applied for that earlier period.

36　　IFRS 3 *Business Combinations* (as revised in 2008) amended paragraphs 19, C1 and C4(f) and (g). If an entity applies IFRS 3 (revised 2008) for an earlier period, the amendments shall also be applied for that earlier period.

37　　IAS 27 *Consolidated and Separate Financial Statements* (as amended in 2008) amended paragraphs B1 and B7. If an entity applies IAS 27 (amended 2008) for an earlier period, the amendments shall be applied for that earlier period.

38　　*Cost of an Investment in a Subsidiary, Jointly Controlled Entity or Associate* (Amendments to IFRS 1 and IAS 27), issued in May 2008, added paragraphs 31, D1(g), D14 and D15. An entity shall apply those paragraphs for annual periods beginning on or after 1 July 2009. Earlier application is permitted. If an entity applies the paragraphs for an earlier period, it shall disclose that fact.

39　　Paragraph B7 was amended by *Improvements to IFRSs* issued in May 2008. An entity shall apply those amendments for annual periods beginning on or after 1 July 2009. If an entity applies IAS 27 (amended 2008) for an earlier period, the amendments shall be applied for that earlier period.

39A   *Additional Exemptions for First-time Adopters* (Amendments to IFRS 1), issued in July 2009, added paragraphs 31A, D8A, D9A and D21A and amended paragraph D1(c), (d) and (l). An entity shall apply those amendments for annual periods beginning on or after 1 January 2010. Earlier application is permitted. If an entity applies the amendments for an earlier period it shall disclose that fact.

39B   [Deleted]

39C   IFRIC 19 *Extinguishing Financial Liabilities with Equity Instruments* added paragraph D25. An entity shall apply that amendment when it applies IFRIC 19.

39D   [Deleted]

39E   *Improvements to IFRSs* issued in May 2010 added paragraphs 27A, 31B and D8B and amended paragraphs 27, 32, D1(c) and D8. An entity shall apply those amendments for annual periods beginning on or after 1 January 2011. Earlier application is permitted. If an entity applies the amendments for an earlier period it shall disclose that fact. Entities that adopted IFRSs in periods before the effective date of IFRS 1 or applied IFRS 1 in a previous period are permitted to apply the amendment to paragraph D8 retrospectively in the first annual period after the amendment is effective. An entity applying paragraph D8 retrospectively shall disclose that fact.

39F   [Deleted]

39G   [Deleted]

39H   *Severe Hyperinflation and Removal of Fixed Dates for First-time Adopters* (Amendments to IFRS 1), issued in December 2010, amended paragraphs B2, D1 and D20 and added paragraphs 31C and D26–D30. An entity shall apply those amendments for annual periods beginning on or after 1 July 2011. Earlier application is permitted.

39I   IFRS 10 *Consolidated Financial Statements* and IFRS 11 *Joint Arrangements*, issued in May 2011, amended paragraphs 31, B7, C1, D1, D14 and D15 and added paragraph D31. An entity shall apply those amendments when it applies IFRS 10 and IFRS 11.

39J   IFRS 13 *Fair Value Measurement*, issued in May 2011, deleted paragraph 19, amended the definition of fair value in Appendix A and amended paragraphs D15 and D20. An entity shall apply those amendments when it applies IFRS 13.

39K   *Presentation of Items of Other Comprehensive Income* (Amendments to IAS 1), issued in June 2011, amended paragraph 21. An entity shall apply that amendment when it applies IAS 1 as amended in June 2011.

39L   IAS 19 *Employee Benefits* (as amended in June 2011) amended paragraph D1 and deleted paragraphs D10 and D11. An entity shall apply those amendments when it applies IAS 19 (as amended in June 2011).

39M   IFRIC 20 *Stripping Costs in the Production Phase of a Surface Mine* added paragraph D32 and amended paragraph D1. An entity shall apply that amendment when it applies IFRIC 20.

39N   *Government Loans* (Amendments to IFRS 1), issued in March 2012, added paragraphs B1(f) and B10–B12. An entity shall apply those paragraphs for annual periods beginning on or after 1 January 2013. Earlier application is permitted.

39O   Paragraphs B10 and B11 refer to IFRS 9. If an entity applies this IFRS but does not yet apply IFRS 9, the references in paragraphs B10 and B11 to IFRS 9 shall be read as references to IAS 39 *Financial Instruments: Recognition and Measurement*.

39P   *Annual Improvements 2009–2011 Cycle*, issued in May 2012, added paragraphs 4A–4B and 23A–23B. An entity shall apply that amendment retrospectively in accordance with IAS 8 *Accounting Policies, Changes in Accounting Estimates and Errors* for annual periods beginning on or after 1 January 2013. Earlier application is permitted. If an entity applies that amendment for an earlier period it shall disclose that fact.

39Q   *Annual Improvements 2009–2011 Cycle*, issued in May 2012, amended paragraph D23. An entity shall apply that amendment retrospectively in accordance with IAS 8 *Accounting Policies, Changes in Accounting Estimates and Errors* for annual periods beginning on or after 1 January 2013. Earlier application is permitted. If an entity applies that amendment for an earlier period it shall disclose that fact.

39R   *Annual Improvements 2009–2011 Cycle*, issued in May 2012, amended paragraph 21. An entity shall apply that amendment retrospectively in accordance with IAS 8 *Accounting Policies, Changes in Accounting Estimates and Errors* for annual periods beginning on or after 1 January 2013. Earlier application is permitted. If an entity applies that amendment for an earlier period it shall disclose that fact.

39S   *Consolidated Financial Statements, Joint Arrangements and Disclosure of Interests in Other Entities: Transition Guidance* (Amendments to IFRS 10, IFRS 11 and IFRS 12), issued in June 2012, amended paragraph D31. An entity shall apply that amendment when it applies IFRS 11 (as amended in June 2012).

39T   *Investment Entities* (Amendments to IFRS 10, IFRS 12 and IAS 27), issued in October 2012, amended paragraphs D16, D17 and Appendix C. An entity shall apply those amendments for annual periods beginning on or after 1 January 2014. Earlier application of *Investment Entities* is permitted. If an entity applies those amendments earlier it shall also apply all amendments included in *Investment Entities* at the same time.

39U   [Deleted]

39V   IFRS 14 *Regulatory Deferral Accounts*, issued in January 2014, amended paragraph D8B. An entity shall apply that amendment for annual periods beginning on or after 1 January 2016. Earlier application is permitted. If an entity applies IFRS 14 for an earlier period, the amendment shall be applied for that earlier period.

39W   *Accounting for Acquisitions of Interests in Joint Operations* (Amendments to IFRS 11), issued in May 2014, amended paragraph C5. An entity shall apply that amendment in annual periods beginning on or after 1 January 2016. If an entity applies related amendments to IFRS 11 from *Accounting for Acquisitions of Interests in Joint Operations* (Amendments to IFRS 11) in an earlier period, the amendment to paragraph C5 shall be applied in that earlier period.

39X   IFRS 15 *Revenue from Contracts with Customers*, issued in May 2014, amended paragraph D1, deleted paragraph D24 and its related heading and added paragraphs D34–D35 and their related heading. An entity shall apply those amendments when it applies IFRS 15.

39Y   IFRS 9 *Financial Instruments*, as issued in July 2014, amended paragraphs 29, B1–B6, D1, D14, D15, D19 and D20, deleted paragraphs 39B, 39G and 39U and added paragraphs 29A, B8–B8G, B9, D19A–D19C, D33, E1 and E2. An entity shall apply those amendments when it applies IFRS 9.

39Z   *Equity Method in Separate Financial Statements* (Amendments to IAS 27), issued in August 2014, amended paragraph D14 and added paragraph D15A. An entity shall apply those amendments for annual periods beginning on or after 1 January 2016. Earlier application is permitted. If an entity applies those amendments for an earlier period, it shall disclose that fact.

39AA   [Deleted]

39AB   IFRS 16 *Leases*, issued in January 2016, amended paragraphs 30, C4, D1, D7, D8B and D9, deleted paragraph D9A and added paragraphs D9B–D9E. An entity shall apply those amendments when it applies IFRS 16.

39AC   IFRIC 22 *Foreign Currency Transactions and Advance Consideration* added paragraph D36 and amended paragraph D1. An entity shall apply that amendment when it applies IFRIC 22.

39AD   *Annual Improvements to IFRS Standards 2014–2016 Cycle*, issued in December 2016, amended paragraphs 39L and 39T and deleted paragraphs 39D, 39F, 39AA and E3–E7. An entity shall apply those amendments for annual periods beginning on or after 1 January 2018.

39AE   *[This paragraph refers to amendments that are not yet effective, and is therefore not included in this edition.]*

39AF   IFRIC 23 *Uncertainty over Income Tax Treatments* added paragraph E8. An entity shall apply that amendment when it applies IFRIC 23.

39AG   *[This paragraph refers to amendments that are not yet effective, and is therefore not included in this edition.]*

Withdrawal of IFRS 1 (issued 2003)

40   This IFRS supersedes IFRS 1 (issued in 2003 and amended at May 2008).

Appendix A
Defined terms

This appendix is an integral part of the IFRS.

date of transition to IFRSs	The beginning of the earliest period for which an entity presents full comparative information under IFRSs in its **first IFRS financial statements**.
deemed cost	An amount used as a surrogate for cost or depreciated cost at a given date. Subsequent depreciation or amortisation assumes that the entity had initially recognised the asset or liability at the given date and that its cost was equal to the deemed cost.
fair value	*Fair value* is the price that would be received to sell an asset or paid to transfer a liability in an orderly transaction between market participants at the measurement date. (See IFRS 13.)
first IFRS financial statements	The first annual financial statements in which an entity adopts **International Financial Reporting Standards (IFRSs)**, by an explicit and unreserved statement of compliance with IFRSs.
first IFRS reporting period	The latest reporting period covered by an entity's **first IFRS financial statements**.
first-time adopter	An entity that presents its **first IFRS financial statements**.
International Financial Reporting Standards (IFRSs)	Standards and Interpretations issued by the International Accounting Standards Board (IASB). They comprise:
	(a) International Financial Reporting Standards;
	(b) International Accounting Standards;
	(c) IFRIC Interpretations; and
	(d) SIC Interpretations.[1]
opening IFRS statement of financial position	An entity's statement of financial position at the **date of transition to IFRSs**.
previous GAAP	The basis of accounting that a **first-time adopter** used immediately before adopting IFRSs.

---

1   Definition of IFRSs amended after the name changes introduced by the revised Constitution of the IFRS Foundation in 2010.

Appendix B
Exceptions to the retrospective application of other IFRSs

This appendix is an integral part of the IFRS.

B1   An entity shall apply the following exceptions:

(a)   derecognition of financial assets and financial liabilities (paragraphs B2 and B3);

(b)   hedge accounting (paragraphs B4–B6);

(c)   non-controlling interests (paragraph B7);

(d)   classification and measurement of financial assets (paragraphs B8–B8C);

(e)   impairment of financial assets (paragraphs B8D–B8G);

(f)   embedded derivatives (paragraph B9); and

(g)   government loans (paragraphs B10–B12).

Derecognition of financial assets and financial liabilities

B2   Except as permitted by paragraph B3, a first-time adopter shall apply the derecognition requirements in IFRS 9 prospectively for transactions occurring on or after the date of transition to IFRSs. For example, if a first-time adopter derecognised non-derivative financial assets or non-derivative financial liabilities in accordance with its previous GAAP as a result of a transaction that occurred before the date of transition to IFRSs, it shall not recognise those assets and liabilities in accordance with IFRSs (unless they qualify for recognition as a result of a later transaction or event).

B3   Despite paragraph B2, an entity may apply the derecognition requirements in IFRS 9 retrospectively from a date of the entity's choosing, provided that the information needed to apply IFRS 9 to financial assets and financial liabilities derecognised as a result of past transactions was obtained at the time of initially accounting for those transactions.

Hedge accounting

B4   As required by IFRS 9, at the date of transition to IFRSs an entity shall:

(a)   measure all derivatives at fair value; and

(b)   eliminate all deferred losses and gains arising on derivatives that were reported in accordance with previous GAAP as if they were assets or liabilities.

B5   An entity shall not reflect in its opening IFRS statement of financial position a hedging relationship of a type that does not qualify for hedge accounting in accordance with IFRS 9 (for example, many hedging relationships where the hedging instrument is a stand-alone written option or a net written option; or where the hedged item is a net position in a cash flow hedge for another risk than foreign currency risk). However, if an entity designated a net position as a hedged item in accordance with previous GAAP, it may designate as a hedged item in accordance with IFRSs an individual item within that net position, or a net position if that meets the requirements in paragraph 6.6.1 of IFRS 9, provided that it does so no later than the date of transition to IFRSs.

B6   If, before the date of transition to IFRSs, an entity had designated a transaction as a hedge but the hedge does not meet the conditions for hedge accounting in IFRS 9, the entity shall apply paragraphs 6.5.6 and 6.5.7 of IFRS 9 to discontinue hedge accounting. Transactions entered into before the date of transition to IFRSs shall not be retrospectively designated as hedges.

Non-controlling interests

B7   A first-time adopter shall apply the following requirements of IFRS 10 prospectively from the date of transition to IFRSs:

(a)   the requirement in paragraph B94 that total comprehensive income is attributed to the owners of the parent and to the non-controlling interests even if this results in the non-controlling interests having a deficit balance;

(b)   the requirements in paragraphs 23 and B96 for accounting for changes in the parent's ownership interest in a subsidiary that do not result in a loss of control; and

(c)   the requirements in paragraphs B97–B99 for accounting for a loss of control over a subsidiary, and the related requirements of paragraph 8A of IFRS 5 *Non-current Assets Held for Sale and Discontinued Operations*.

However, if a first-time adopter elects to apply IFRS 3 retrospectively to past business combinations, it shall also apply IFRS 10 in accordance with paragraph C1 of this IFRS.

Classification and measurement of financial instruments

B8   An entity shall assess whether a financial asset meets the conditions in paragraph 4.1.2 of IFRS 9 or the conditions in paragraph 4.1.2A of IFRS 9 on the basis of the facts and circumstances that exist at the date of transition to IFRSs.

B8A   If it is impracticable to assess a modified time value of money element in accordance with paragraphs B4.1.9B–B4.1.9D of IFRS 9 on the basis of the facts and circumstances that exist at the date of transition to IFRSs, an entity shall assess the contractual cash flow characteristics of that financial asset on the basis of the facts and circumstances that existed at the date of transition to IFRSs without taking into account the requirements related to the modification of the time value of money element in paragraphs B4.1.9B–B4.1.9D of IFRS 9. (In this case, the entity shall also apply paragraph 42R of IFRS 7 but references to 'paragraph 7.2.4 of IFRS 9' shall be read to mean this paragraph and references to 'initial recognition of the financial asset' shall be read to mean 'at the date of transition to IFRSs'.)

B8B If it is impracticable to assess whether the fair value of a prepayment feature is insignificant in accordance with paragraph B4.1.12(c) of IFRS 9 on the basis of the facts and circumstances that exist at the date of transition to IFRSs, an entity shall assess the contractual cash flow characteristics of that financial asset on the basis of the facts and circumstances that existed at the date of transition to IFRSs without taking into account the exception for prepayment features in paragraph B4.1.12 of IFRS 9. (In this case, the entity shall also apply paragraph 42S of IFRS 7 but references to 'paragraph 7.2.5 of IFRS 9' shall be read to mean this paragraph and references to 'initial recognition of the financial asset' shall be read to mean 'at the date of transition to IFRSs'.)

B8C If it is impracticable (as defined in IAS 8) for an entity to apply retrospectively the effective interest method in IFRS 9, the fair value of the financial asset or the financial liability at the date of transition to IFRSs shall be the new gross carrying amount of that financial asset or the new amortised cost of that financial liability at the date of transition to IFRSs.

Impairment of financial assets

B8D An entity shall apply the impairment requirements in Section 5.5 of IFRS 9 retrospectively subject to paragraphs B8E–B8G and E1–E2.

B8E At the date of transition to IFRSs, an entity shall use reasonable and supportable information that is available without undue cost or effort to determine the credit risk at the date that financial instruments were initially recognised (or for loan commitments and financial guarantee contracts the date that the entity became a party to the irrevocable commitment in accordance with paragraph 5.5.6 of IFRS 9) and compare that to the credit risk at the date of transition to IFRSs (also see paragraphs B7.2.2–B7.2.3 of IFRS 9).

B8F When determining whether there has been a significant increase in credit risk since initial recognition, an entity may apply:

(a) the requirements in paragraph 5.5.10 and B5.5.22–B5.5.24 of IFRS 9; and

(b) the rebuttable presumption in paragraph 5.5.11 of IFRS 9 for contractual payments that are more than 30 days past due if an entity will apply the impairment requirements by identifying significant increases in credit risk since initial recognition for those financial instruments on the basis of past due information.

B8G If, at the date of transition to IFRSs, determining whether there has been a significant increase in credit risk since the initial recognition of a financial instrument would require undue cost or effort, an entity shall recognise a loss allowance at an amount equal to lifetime expected credit losses at each reporting date until that financial instrument is derecognised (unless that financial instrument is low credit risk at a reporting date, in which case paragraph B8F(a) applies).

Embedded derivatives

B9   A first-time adopter shall assess whether an embedded derivative is required to be separated from the host contract and accounted for as a derivative on the basis of the conditions that existed at the later of the date it first became a party to the contract and the date a reassessment is required by paragraph B4.3.11 of IFRS 9.

Government loans

B10   A first-time adopter shall classify all government loans received as a financial liability or an equity instrument in accordance with IAS 32 *Financial Instruments: Presentation*. Except as permitted by paragraph B11, a first-time adopter shall apply the requirements in IFRS 9 *Financial Instruments* and IAS 20 *Accounting for Government Grants and Disclosure of Government Assistance* prospectively to government loans existing at the date of transition to IFRSs and shall not recognise the corresponding benefit of the government loan at a below-market rate of interest as a government grant. Consequently, if a first-time adopter did not, under its previous GAAP, recognise and measure a government loan at a below-market rate of interest on a basis consistent with IFRS requirements, it shall use its previous GAAP carrying amount of the loan at the date of transition to IFRSs as the carrying amount of the loan in the opening IFRS statement of financial position. An entity shall apply IFRS 9 to the measurement of such loans after the date of transition to IFRSs.

B11   Despite paragraph B10, an entity may apply the requirements in IFRS 9 and IAS 20 retrospectively to any government loan originated before the date of transition to IFRSs, provided that the information needed to do so had been obtained at the time of initially accounting for that loan.

B12   The requirements and guidance in paragraphs B10 and B11 do not preclude an entity from being able to use the exemptions described in paragraphs D19–D19C relating to the designation of previously recognised financial instruments at fair value through profit or loss.

B13   *[This paragraph refers to amendments that are not yet effective, and is therefore not included in this edition.]*

Appendix C
Exemptions for business combinations

This appendix is an integral part of the IFRS. An entity shall apply the following requirements to business combinations that the entity recognised before the date of transition to IFRSs. This Appendix should only be applied to business combinations within the scope of IFRS 3 Business Combinations.

C1 A first-time adopter may elect not to apply IFRS 3 retrospectively to past business combinations (business combinations that occurred before the date of transition to IFRSs). However, if a first-time adopter restates any business combination to comply with IFRS 3, it shall restate all later business combinations and shall also apply IFRS 10 from that same date. For example, if a first-time adopter elects to restate a business combination that occurred on 30 June 20X6, it shall restate all business combinations that occurred between 30 June 20X6 and the date of transition to IFRSs, and it shall also apply IFRS 10 from 30 June 20X6.

C2 An entity need not apply IAS 21 *The Effects of Changes in Foreign Exchange Rates* retrospectively to fair value adjustments and goodwill arising in business combinations that occurred before the date of transition to IFRSs. If the entity does not apply IAS 21 retrospectively to those fair value adjustments and goodwill, it shall treat them as assets and liabilities of the entity rather than as assets and liabilities of the acquiree. Therefore, those goodwill and fair value adjustments either are already expressed in the entity's functional currency or are non-monetary foreign currency items, which are reported using the exchange rate applied in accordance with previous GAAP.

C3 An entity may apply IAS 21 retrospectively to fair value adjustments and goodwill arising in either:

(a) all business combinations that occurred before the date of transition to IFRSs; or

(b) all business combinations that the entity elects to restate to comply with IFRS 3, as permitted by paragraph C1 above.

C4 If a first-time adopter does not apply IFRS 3 retrospectively to a past business combination, this has the following consequences for that business combination:

(a) The first-time adopter shall keep the same classification (as an acquisition by the legal acquirer, a reverse acquisition by the legal acquiree, or a uniting of interests) as in its previous GAAP financial statements.

(b) The first-time adopter shall recognise all its assets and liabilities at the date of transition to IFRSs that were acquired or assumed in a past business combination, other than:

(i) some financial assets and financial liabilities derecognised in accordance with previous GAAP (see paragraph B2); and